Tales of a Tail Gunner:
A Memoir of Seattle and World War II

Eddie S. Picardo

Published by
Hara Publishing
P.O. Box 19732
Seattle, WA 98109
206-775-7868

First printing, 1996
Second printing, 1997, revised

ISBN: 1-883697-33-6

Library of Congress Catalog Card Number: 96-77149

Editor: Margaret Smith
Copy Editor: Victoria McCown
Desktop Publishing: Shael Anderson
Cover Design: Ron de Wilde
Back Cover Photo: Tim Schlecht

I have tried to be accurate and diligent in my research. Please excuse any factual inaccuracies due to inadvertence, not lack of effort.

<u>Dedication</u>

To my beloved Grandmother
Amelia De Tore
Who put the fear of God in me

To my beloved brother
Robert F. Picardo
my very best friend

And to all the boys
who never made it home

Acknowledgements

Louise Kennedy
who urged me for years to write a book

Edgar J. Spencer
John Beavers
Tom Stewart
Gerald A. Polzin
Daryl Ogden
Margaret Smith
Dean and Georgie Guintoli
Steve and Linda Kaufer
Donna Picardo
Joe and Alice Mariani
Bob Picardo II
Norma Vangelos
Tim and Joyce Stensen
Lorraine Stensen
Georgina Picardo
Mary Picardo
Helene Mitchell(Mitch the Bitch)
Mrs. Mary Alice Strom
Greg Spurck
Bob Stewart
Diane Talley
Gina Vangelos
Ernie Merlino
Tony Caruso

Hara Publishing Group
Sheryn Hara
Karla Kombrink

Table of Contents

PRELUDE

Life in Seattle,
Death over Germany,
Life (and Death) in England

In 1944, the combined air forces of the United States and Great Britain began bombing oil refineries inside Germany. By targeting oil refineries, the bigwig military strategists hoped to cripple Germany's war effort and hasten the end of World War II. Sounds like a good idea, right? Well, it sounds good if you're not on one of the bomber crews sent to blow up one of those heavily defended refineries to kingdom come.

If you know someone who helped destroy a German oil refinery, then you know someone who has been to hell and back. As a B-24 tail gunner during the War, I made the round trip journey plenty of times. And let me tell you, when our plane landed back on English soil after the first refinery bombing mission, I could never have predicted that I would be here to write about it fifty years later.

Our crew's first oil refinery was in Hamburg, on the coast of the North Sea. That meant we didn't have to fly over Germany for too long, but it did mean that we had to fly through a blanket of flak and a hoard of screaming German fighters in order to drop our payload. I don't think any of us had imagined how fiercely the Germans would defend their oil refineries. But the Nazis understood that with the twentieth century's mechanized brand of warfare, oil was a country's lifeblood. They couldn't stand by and just let us bleed them to death. So they fought like hell. In 1944 alone German flak destroyed 3,501 American Aircraft.

As we approached the Hamburg oil refinery, we hit what was called the Initial Point, or IP. At that moment, we turned toward the target, our fighter support peeled off from the bomber formation, and our plane's radio operator opened up the huge bomb bay doors. The German air defense teams tracked us with flak from their deadly 88 millimeter anti-aircraft guns. We wore flak jackets of heavy fabric containing metal plates to protect us from the shrapnel of their exploding shells. When we arrived directly over the refinery, a huge barrage of flak engulfed our B-24. The flak was so thick it blotted out the sun. There might as well have been a full eclipse for more than ten seconds. I thought it was all over for me and my buddies. "Good night, sweetheart," I muttered to myself.

But somehow we dropped our bomb load, banked to the left and got the hell out of the target area. A minute or two later, we picked up our fighter escorts and headed for "home" — England. The B-24 was pockmarked with holes and had sustained some serious damage—we had lost our number four engine, flak had cut its oil lines. Miraculously, no one on our crew was hurt.

When we landed, I started talking to myself. Only an intercom system allowed us to communicate with our crew in the B-24, but I didn't need an intercom system to hear myself talk, or to read the writing on the wall. "There's no way I will live through this," I remember saying. "There is no way." Yet after volunteering for the Air Force shortly after Pearl Harbor, I knew I couldn't bug out before my time—I had a commitment to my country and to my crew to stick it out until the end.

And the end of the War didn't seem very far away for me at all. After one or two more oil refinery missions, I figured I would be history, blown up into a thousand pieces in the skies over Germany. I was just a bit player in the biggest morality play ever put on, starring Hitler, Goehring, Himmler and Goebbels on the Nazi side, the greatest group of nasties ever assembled; opposed by Roosevelt, Churchill, Eisenhower and Montgomery on the Allies' side. The life of Eddie Picardo, a first-generation Italian-American from Seattle, didn't (to paraphrase Bogart in Casablanca) amount to a hill of beans next to world history in the making. Except to me, Eddie Picardo. And my family.

Flying combat missions over Germany was strictly voluntary. I could have quit any time I wanted to. But once I started something, I could never quit. I still can't quit anything I start today; that's just the way I am. But dumb as I might have been to volunteer to be a tail gunner, I wasn't so dumb as not to pay six dollars and fifty cents a month out of my paycheck for military life insurance. That way, if I got killed—which seemed very likely, especially after my first trip to Hamburg—my family would at least receive ten thousand dollars in compensation.

When my feet touched the ground after Hamburg, they felt a little wobbly. But as soon as I could almost walk straight, I scouted out the first sergeant. "I want the Army to take out thirteen dollars from my paycheck instead of six-fifty," I told him, "because I want to be insured for twenty thousand."

He looked at me kind of funny, then scowled, "You can't do that."

I said, "It's my money, I can do anything I want with it." But he insisted that ten thousand dollars was the honest-to-God, absolute military ceiling on insurance. Well, in those days, when someone told me I couldn't do something I had decided to do, I got mad. Too much Italian blood in my veins, I suspect. But it didn't matter how hot or disappointed I got, I wasn't going to win an argument with the military, Italian passion or not.

So I resorted to another kind of time-honored life insurance: the rosary. I had learned the rosary in Seattle from my grandmother. During Lent she made my grandfather and me recite five decades of the rosary every night. For the rest of the war, each night before I was assigned to a bombing mission, I would recite five decades of the rosary, just as I had done as a boy growing up in Seattle. Someone said once that there are no atheists in foxholes. Well, I'm here to tell you that there aren't any atheists in the tail of a B-24, either.

My family never got ten thousand bucks for me during the war, but at least they got to see me again. My father may have wished he had gotten the money instead. But after flying thirty-three missions over Germany and France without getting my butt blown out of the sky, I was only too happy to return to Seattle with three hundred dollars, my military severance pay, considerably less than an insurance check underwritten by the United States Air Force. So I guess my monthly insurance payment helped some other young GI who had the misfortune of dying while protecting the tail of a B-24 Liberator. It could just as easily have been me.

The First Picardos in Seattle

If you ever come to Seattle, just north of the University District in an area of town called Ravenna, you will be surprised to discover, on the corner of 25th Avenue NE and 82nd Street, the Picardo Pea Patch. Community pea patches—cooperative gardening efforts— are located all over Seattle, and in the most unexpected places. For my money, this one's the best. But I'm a little biased, of course.

The Picardo Pea Patch owes its name, as you might expect, to my family. The first two Picardoin Seattleites were Ernesto and Costandine, who initially stopped at Boston near the turn of the century. If they had stayed there, they would no doubt have lived in one of the busy Italian neighborhoods of the North End. But they only remained in Boston for a short while, deciding to travel across the wide United States. During their journey they found an immense, modern country, very different from their rustic, spaghetti-thin Italy, where most people never traveled more than twenty or thirty miles from their birthplace. What a different life these Picardos would lead from their ancestors!

These boys, hard workers both, courted Italian girls in the long-distance Italian way, through intensive written negotiations and offers of marriage. Finally, both received the parental blessing, but they had to wait many months for their fiancées to arrive in Seattle. These couples produced the first American-born Italian children in the family. These Picardo boys came to love America, but they might have loved Italian girls a little bit more— they would never have dreamed of marrying Americans.

The Picardos made a mostly Italian life for themselves in America. They bought a large farm, cultivated it at first with Italian techniques, then with more modern American methods. They played bocce ball, drank red wine during Prohibition, and, before long, described themselves and their children as Italian-Americans. As a result of this successful bit of cultural assimilation, I grew up celebrating the Fourth of July with all the enthusiasm of a New Englander descended from the Mayflower.

Much of the old Picardo farm is gone now, replaced with houses, but some of it is still in use, divided into dozens of small parcels and worked by neighborhood residents. When I go to look at it, which is rare these days, I still picture the stooped-over figures of my family, tending the soil that nurtured the Picardos during our first decades in the New World. It must have seemed to those Picardos that anything was possible.

In fact, anything was so possible in Seattle in the years just after World War I that around 1925 the Picardos, prospering from their labors on the farm, were able to buy a house called "The Bagley Mansion," near beautiful Green Lake, just about a mile west of the Picardo farm. It was named for Bagley Street, not because the Bagleys, well-known early Seattle settlers, actually lived there. Like everyone else in my family, I grew up calling the mansion simply, "The Big House."

Ernesto

The patriarch of our family was Ernesto Picardo, my grandmother's brother. He was one of the two boys who had originally made good from Italy. He lived in The Big House and everyone called him "The Boss" because his opinions came out of his mouth like pronouncements. Nobody dared cross Ernesto. I resented Ernesto, though, because I had come to believe that only my grandmother could tell me what to do, not some self-important clan leader.

I did anything I could to drive him crazy, which I managed to do a lot. Some of that boyish ornery attitude, fostered by my resentment of Ernesto, sure paid off for me when we were bombing the bejesus out of those oil refineries. You've got to be more than a little onery to volunteer for duty as a tail gunner. Probably a little crazy and maybe a little stupid, too, but mostly ornery and tough. Living near Ernesto made me both.

I grew up mostly with my grandparents. We lived in the shadow of The Big House, in a white stucco Mediterranean-style house. Built under the influence of Ernesto and The Big House, three other satellite houses for members of the Picardo clan were sprinkled within a block of one another. With the exception of The Big House, ours was the nicest of them all. Those houses still stand today.

During the 1920s, nothing but trees and open space surrounded the Picardo residential property. Today almost all of the property has been bought up. Strangers, whose names don't bear any resemblance to Italian names, live there. The access road and driveway to the Big House tells me it's for private transportation only, off limits to trespassers. It feels strange to be denied entrance to the Big House, the place where so much of my growing up took place. When I visited there recently for a look, I half-expected to see Ernesto standing at his office window upstairs, looking down on me and wondering what mischief I had been up to. I would have given anything to see that grand old son-of-a-bitch again.

These days, as I put my memories of Seattle and World War II down on paper, I notice that The Big House and the other Picardo homes are surrounded by typical Seattle middle-class houses. None of these houses can hold a candle to The Big House. If you ever take the trouble to travel to 2200 North 77th Street, almost directly north of Green Lake, you can still imagine the pride that came from being a member of the Picardo clan in the twenties and thirties. If ever there was an American immigrant success story, this was it. In the following pages I'm going to do my best to capture a series of snapshots of that time, to describe what it was like to eat frittata, to stomp on grapes during Prohibition, and to become a Northwestern American with a distinctly Italian flavor. This is a memoir about the Picardo legacy, a rich and vivid picture of pre-World War II Seattle, a violent and exciting account of World War II England and Germany.

Life (and Death) in England

During one of my trips to London, I was sitting in a club with one of my crew members. A girl backed up her chair and hit mine. She apologized and said, "I'm sorry, Yank."

I looked at her and replied, "That's OK. You're not leaving are you?"

She said, "No, I'm just going to the powder room."

I smiled, "Can I come in and watch?"

She gave me a weird look and began laughing. "No, I can manage." I asked if she would be interested in a game of darts when she came back.

She said, "I would like that, Yank."

It was pretty funny for me, an Italian-American from Seattle, to be called "Yank," but I loved it, especially with her English accent. It made me feel like even more of a Yank than I really was.

When she returned we started playing darts. I didn't really care much about darts, but I enjoyed watching it because the British took it so seriously and played so well. And I especially liked watching this woman play. Within a few minutes I had forgotten all about the guys I was with, even my flight buddy. That kind of behavior was common back then, because we never knew which day might be our last. We lived for the moment and never passed up a chance to spend some time with a beautiful woman. And let me tell you, Becky was beautiful.

In my day, if a girl was beautiful you called her a "tomato." If she had a nice figure you would say she was "built like a brick shithouse." Boy oh boy, she had both a beautiful face and figure. I knew I was one lucky bastard to be throwing darts with her.

I felt like I needed some kind of a line to impress her so I told her that I was from North Hollywood. I felt comfortable with this lie because I had met a guy during my training at Las Vegas, New Mexico who actually was from North Hollywood. His father owned a small cafe where movie stars would go to escape being hounded by reporters and fans. This guy had some big names there, like Lana Turner and Errol Flynn, just about the two biggest stars of the time.

There is no adequate way to describe the way English girls felt about Hollywood. All of them thought that if they were beautiful and could get to Hollywood somehow, they could become movie stars. I don't know if Becky thought she could become a movie star, but I felt like I was talking to a potential Hollywood starlet when I looked into her gorgeous eyes. Now that was living!

Becky was absolutely fascinated by my North Hollywood origins. She asked me how far my dad's café was from Hollywood itself. I was dumbfounded for a second or two, but without much hesitation said, "One block." She seemed impressed, and I felt like my chances were improving.

After throwing darts for about half an hour, I told her it was my first trip to London, which was as much a lie as my saying I was from North Hollywood. I told her I would love to see the sights. In those days if you were a flyer, you would get your basic pay plus flight pay, which meant guys like me had money to spend on girls like Becky.

Now, you have to remember that by 1944, England had already been hard at war with Germany for five years and had been through a lot. English citizens were aching for entertaining diversions, and more than a few English girls latched on to American soldiers to show them a good time. So I guess Becky latched onto me for that reason.

Maybe in the back of her mind she thought she might end up back in North Hollywood and be discovered by a talent scout. But young people in those days didn't let opportunities pass them by. We seized every one we could. I think that's why Becky and I seized upon each other.

That day we went to see Buckingham Palace, Big Ben, Tower Bridge, and Number 10 Downing Street. We walked all over the bombed-out city and saw what was left of its monuments. As evening wore on, she told me that she had to be at her office job early the next morning. She said that she would invite me to her flat if she could, but her landlady didn't allow men in the building, especially members of the American military. Becky couldn't afford to get in trouble with her landlady, so I gave her the address of my base and told her to write me so that we could get together again.

To be in Norwich by midnight I had to take the 5:00 p.m. train out of Victoria Station. But I had enjoyed the evening so much that I took the midnight train, which got me on the base around 7:00 a.m. The first sergeant caught me and chewed me out, warning me never do such a thing again.

A few days later I received a letter from Becky, and some time after that I finally managed to get another pass to London. Four weeks later, we met in the lobby of the Picadilly Hotel in the heart of London. I was absolutely thrilled to see her. She was as beautiful as ever. Although she had to work in an office until 4:00 p.m. every day, we spent three wonderful evenings together going to clubs, dining, dancing and making love in a London hotel. In the middle of all the death and destruction of war, we were living as intensely as possible. It was exhilarating. Life and death had collided, and life seemed to be winning. Although the clock was ticking, we did our best not to notice. I remember our first night together, hugging on the bed. I told her, "You're about to be kissed by a tail gunner with pork chop lips!"

She smiled and said, "Don't keep me waiting."

"I'm going to put a smile on your face that will last you the rest of your life," I told her. I didn't know at the time how right I might have been.

I never met anyone in England who, sooner or later, didn't have a tragic story to share. Becky was no exception. She told me that she had married someone to whom her brother had introduced her when she was eighteen. He was in the RAF, a pilot of a Hurricane fighter, first cousin of the more famous Spitfire. He was stationed in North Africa, flying in direct support of Montgomery's 8th Army, which somehow was driving back Rommel's desert divisions. One day Becky's Hurricane husband was flying low, strafing German troops, when his plane was hit. It crashed into the ground and exploded. There was no reason to ask if anyone had lived through the crash. I knew the answer only too well from so many of my buddies meeting the same end. I didn't know what to say. He had probably carried a picture of her around with him everywhere. Boy, I know I would have carried her picture if I had been lucky enough to be her husband. I hope he looked at her photo one last time before he got in his fighter the day he died. There was nothing to say to Becky except that I was sorry. I thought to myself, "Who knows? I could be next." And I could have been.

To follow the rules of my pass to the letter, I should have taken that 5:00 p.m. train back to Norwich. But I was just having too good a time with Becky to leave so early. I said, "What the hell? They can't do anything worse than put me up in the tail of a B-24 and fly over an oil refinery. I'll take my chances with the punishment, but I just can't say good-bye yet to Becky." I had decided to spend three evenings with Becky rather than two. That still wouldn't be enough, but it would be better than cutting short our time together.

That evening we went out to a Jewish restaurant, down some steep stairs to a very small dining room. I can still remember what we had for dinner because there was only one item on the menu. We had chicken soup, a piece of boiled chicken with potatoes and Brussels sprouts. I noticed a beautiful display of Danish pastries and couldn't pass it up. We ordered some, but when we bit into them, it was like eating sand. They were sugarless, because sugar was a valuable commodity for the war effort, and people still couldn't get it on the streets of London. We were both terribly disappointed, but Becky blamed herself for not remembering that sugar was impossible to obtain.

We went back to the hotel. Eleven o'clock rolled around, and I really had to catch my train back to

Norwich. There was a perpetual blackout in London to protect everyone from the German bombing raids, even though German offensive air power had become confined to rocket warfare. All we could hear on the streets of London was the clicking of shoes against the pavements. The last thing Becky said was, "I'll write to you as soon as I can."

We smiled at one another, hugged and said goodbye. She left the hotel before me and turned down the street to the right. I left about half a minute after her and turned down the street in the opposite direction. All of a sudden, with no warning, a V-2 rocket exploded nearby. V-2 rockets were faster than sound, so there was never any warning that they were coming in, as there was with the V-1 buzz bombs. The explosion lit up the entire sky—it seemed like daylight for more than a few seconds. I fell flat on my back and looked up to see one side of the Picadilly Hotel weaving back and forth. I got up and ran as fast as I could away from the building. It gradually turned dark again and I ran right smack into a wooden bike rack, tearing my pants and bruising my knees. Those were the only injuries I suffered from the V-2 rocket.

Amid all the confusion, I somehow managed to get to Victoria Station and catch the midnight train back to my base. I arrived once again around 7:00 a.m. and, sure enough, almost like clockwork, there was the first sergeant waiting to greet me. "Picardo, you are a complete mess! I warned you already about coming back late on passes. You are busted. As of now, you are Private Picardo." In the wink of an eye I had been demoted from staff sergeant to buck private.

I got myself cleaned up and went directly to see my pilot, Edgar Spencer. I told him that I refused to fly tail gunner as a private and that I was through with bombing Germany. From now on our crew would have to fight the war without me. Because flying combat missions was a voluntary role, the Air Force could demote me, but they couldn't force me up into the air. Spencer glared at me with his most disgusted look—and believe me, that was a sight to scare you.

Edgar Spencer was a sharp, strict gentleman. He expected absolute perfection out of his crew, and he damn near got it, which is probably why we all made it out of the war alive. He knew every single element and task of the crew's duty like the back of his hand. After I informed Edgar that my time with the crew was over, he got dressed and went to see Colonel Snavely, commander of the 44th bombing group. Within the hour, I had been promoted to staff sergeant again. I often wondered if Edgar got my rating back because I was the only member of the crew that would fly in the tail. Or maybe I was as good a tail gunner as he was a pilot—which would have made me the best tail gunner in the whole 8th Air Force.

I never heard from Becky again. There was no way for me to contact her because I had never seen her flat. I knew she worked in an office, but I never really found out where and I could hardly start looking for her without a clue about where to start in mammoth London. She had put her return address on the mail she sent me early on in our relationship, but I never kept the envelopes after I wrote back. I waited and waited, keeping my eye on the mail delivery every day, but she disappeared altogether from my life. I often wondered if the V-2 that had just missed me had gotten her instead. How tragic it would have been if she died just because I wanted to spend one more evening with her instead of returning to base when I should have. The thirty seconds she left before me might have made all the difference. Who knows? I heard later that the V-2 had exploded two blocks away from the Picadilly Hotel. I wonder if Becky still had a smile on her face.

CHAPTER ONE

Growing Up
with the Picardo Clan

Grandma's Frittata

Whenever I was frightened enough on the B-24 to recite the rosary, I invariably thought of my grandmother. Grandmother raised me until I was fourteen. This was because my mother became quite ill after I was born in 1922. When I was just sixteen months old, my brother Bob was born. Eventually, Mother had three more children, Lorraine, Norma and Jack, but because of her continued frailty, I remained with my grandmother.

Grandmother was born in Italy. She and everyone else in my family came from a small town about forty miles from Naples called Avelino. Grandmother came to America two years after Ernesto arrived in the South Park area of Seattle and sent for his brothers and sisters to join him. Later, he sent for his parents.

Like other Italian women of her generation, she was a staunch Catholic. Although I wasn't technically required to attend Mass on Sundays, the chances of me getting my head knocked off by my grandmother improved considerably if I didn't. So more often than not, I went to Mass. During Lent, saying the rosary wasn't optional for either my grandfather or me. By the time I found myself in a B-24 bomber a decade and a half later, I didn't have any trouble reciting the rosary. I owe that to my grandmother.

My grandparents had a radio, which in the 1930s was our main link to the big world. On Saturday mornings, Grandpa would turn it on to listen to the Metropolitan Opera broadcast its performances from New York City. He would turn the volume up so high that the whole neighborhood didn't have any choice but to listen to it, too, for the three-hour show. I absolutely hated it, partly because I could never understand what all the loud singing was about, and partly because it seemed crazy to sing your way through life. Looking back, it was just about the only thing Grandfather ever did to make me really angry. But he <u>did</u> do it every Saturday. I don't have much more to say about my grandfather because he was emotionally removed from us. He was the type of man who would wolf down dinner and be in bed twenty minutes later. Alone together most nights, my grandmother and I became very close and dependent upon one another. My grandmother was at once a very kind, compassionate woman and yet extremely strict. She was probably the single most important figure in my life.

In those days, Catholics couldn't eat meat on Fridays, so my grandmother made frittata for dinner. To make a frittata, grandmother would pour some olive oil in a frying pan, cut up whatever vegetables were available, and cook them in the oil for a minute or two. After the vegetables just barely began to crisp and brown, she would beat together three eggs and add them to the vegetables. Our next door neighbor, Dr. Beamis, eventually found out about Friday-night frittata. He would come over and ask my grandmother to make one for him. His favorite was asparagus.

I remember Dr. Beamis almost drooling with a big smile on his face, holding a glass of wine in his hand and watching Grandmother's every step in the kitchen as she cooked frittata. When the frittata arrived at the table, the doctor would eat extra slowly and offer up his philosophy of dining at Grandmother's, "The longer it takes to eat it, the better it's going to taste." Let me tell you something, the doctor loved frittata a lot more than I did. I ate it, but I wasn't crazy about it. It's funny to me today to discover that today lots of Italian joints sell frittata as a delicacy — to me frittata was just plain old everyday food.

When finished, Dr. Beamis would visit with us for a while and as he finally got up and left he would say without fail, "See you next Friday, Amy." I couldn't understand why he called her Amy when her name was Amelia. Amy or Amelia, we always saw Dr. Beamis every Friday—he was a man of his word. My grandmother enjoyed cooking for him immensely. It pleased her that he complimented her frittata so much.

My feelings toward frittata are best captured by my experiences with it at Fairview Grade School on 79th and Roosevelt Way in North Seattle. For lunch, grandmother used to make me a frittata sandwich with garlic. I used to look longingly at the other kids with bologna or peanut butter and jelly sandwiches. Oh, how I wanted to trade my frittata sandwich for one of theirs! It took me a long time to realize that I was an Italian-American, and not just an Italian. Maybe it wasn't part of my American destiny to love frittata like Grandma said all of my relatives had. Even before I tasted one, I knew I would like peanut butter and jelly sandwiches more than my native frittata. As a first generation Italian-American, I guess I was culturally assimilated before I even knew what the term meant.

Better than frittata was Grandmother's chicken. I can still almost taste how delicious it was. Since Grandmother left us, I've never experienced chicken like that again. We had a little rock fireplace in the backyard and, when weather permitted, Grandmother would put a huge pan of water over the fire and wait for it to boil.

Then she would walk to the chicken coop a few yards away, grab a chicken, wring its neck, chop its head off with a hatchet and then throw it up in the air. Its wings would flap quite a bit before it hit the ground and there would be a little bit of blood around. After repeating this technique on three or four chickens, she would put them into the boiling water for about a minute, retrieve them and then begin to pull the feathers off. After disrobing the chickens of their feathers, she would open and clean them. A little while later we would eat the freshest, tastiest chicken ever conceived in a kitchen. Witnessing the way Grandmother killed and prepared chickens, with a brutal, no-questions-asked efficiency, I feared nothing. What could possibly happen to me as long as Grandmother was there?

During the winter months, there wasn't much to do on the farm. When it wasn't raining or the ground wasn't frozen, the men would do a little plowing and fertilize some of the planting ground, but there was plenty of spare time. Sometimes seven or eight of the men relatives would meet at Grandmother's house for a game of cards.

When that happened, Grandma would prepare a huge pizza for the men to snack on after the card game...and what a snack! She'd bake bread dough on a large pan. When it was three-quarters baked and about an inch and a half thick, she would take it from the oven and pour virgin olive oil over it. Then came our own canned tomatoes that were taken off the vine and canned when they were dead ripe. Oh, what flavor! She would sprinkle diced onion, a touch of hot peppers, oregano and basil. Finally, she would add homemade sausages and a touch of salt. Back into the oven it went.

When that pizza came out of the oven, the card game would stop cold. The smell of that pizza was all it took. It would be served with wine or coffee royale. To me, the taste of just the dough itself was good enough. I have never tasted pizza like that since. *"Delicioso!"*

Holidays

On holidays, Grandmother and I weren't left to our own devices. We celebrated by eating a mammoth dinner with the rest of the family at the Big House. I can remember Mr. Gai himself, the founder of Gai's Bakery in Seattle, coming over to the house to deliver French bread for a nickel a loaf. Instead of putting the bread in a bag, Gai delivered it the old-fashioned way by sprinkling flour on it.

Holiday dinners lasted forever, beginning with antipasto and soup, followed by spaghetti and meatballs, and climaxed with a chicken or roast accompanied with three or four vegetables like savory cabbage, potatoes, beans and, as always, hot peppers. Green salad appeared, continental style, at the end of dinner. Finally, homemade pies, cookies and cakes emerged from the kitchen along with roasted chestnuts and fruit. Although I don't remember anyone ever getting drunk, the wine flowed, and no one paid any attention to the clock. Nothing else mattered except the company of family and the food on the table. This is what I would call a true feast. It took an extremely long time for the women to store the food and clean up afterwards. In those days, the men would never dream of helping.

The only deviation from this main course menu occurred on Christmas Eve, when Grandmother would make spaghetti sauce with inkfish (today they call it calamari or squid). This would be our main course. Grandmother used to wash it in the sink, which would get so dirty that it would make me sick. Sometimes she would make spaghetti sauce with dried mushrooms, which on the spaghetti reminded me of worms. I wouldn't touch it. All that Italian stuff I hated when I was a kid I love today. Maybe my Italian taste buds have finally caught up with me.

During the winter months, Green Lake would freeze over. Nowadays the lake doesn't freeze solid, because tall trees have grown up around it, protecting it from the cold. I remember the police would drive their motorcycles over the ice to see if it was solid enough to ice skate on. Watching them from the shores of Green Lake, I was concerned. I thought for sure those cycles would break through the ice, but they never did. Sometimes we would go down to the lake in the early evening and build bonfires along the shore, roasting marshmallows and watching people ice skate.

The Big House

Everything in our family revolved around activity at the Big House. Compared to all the other, smaller family houses which surrounded it, the Big House had an enormous kitchen, much bigger than kitchens which you find in homes today. The Big House kitchen produced some amazing meals during my childhood. Adjoining the kitchen was a large pantry that was as big as a good-sized bedroom. That pantry held an enormous amount of food.

Near the kitchen was the family dining room. In one corner, Ernesto's desk stood with his spittoon next to it on one side and a davenport on the other. The dining room had a large oval table that seated about twenty people.

As big as it was, the family dining room was dwarfed by the formal dining room. This room seated about thirty-five people and was filled with mahogany furniture. From this room you could walk into the living room, which was much smaller than the dining room. A sliding glass door divided the dining and living rooms from one another.

The living room was decorated in red velvet drapes and had a large fireplace with carved mahogany wood and a copper canopy. Two davenports, five large chairs, and a long coffee table, all built from mahogany, were arranged around the room surrounded by floor lamps that were set up in an inviting fashion. That room was so comfortable!

I loved it. Every Christmas the Picardo clan would bring in the biggest Christmas tree that I've ever seen in a private home.

The stairway to the upstairs was also carved mahogany woodwork. On the second floor were four large bedrooms with one master bedroom, and a huge bathroom covered entirely in tile. Here was located the only bathtub, shower and toilet in the entire house! A long, old-fashioned metal chain descended from the toilet tank. A balcony off the master bedroom faced out toward Green Lake. Outside the master bedroom was another set of stairs leading up to the ballroom where the Picardos held enormous dancing parties.

When Sam Picardo, Ernesto's eldest son, married Mary Isernio on April 10, 1926, the wedding was followed by a reception in the Picardo ballroom. It was the first official reception ever held there. Rosaia Brothers Florist decorated the stairways all the way up to the ballroom with white ribbon and flowers. The women got together and cooked all the food, which was served in the formal dining room. There was dancing with live music. Beer and wine were served in the ballroom. It was a terrific way to inaugurate the family ballroom.

Wine During Prohibition

During Prohibition, my family used to make its own wine. My God, you couldn't ask a group of Italian immigrants not to drink wine! Wine, especially red wine, practically courses through Italian veins. As I remember, Prohibition dictated that if you were caught making wine for your own consumption, you were fined. But if you made wine and tried to sell it, you were thrown into jail with no questions asked. At that point, you became a bootlegger.

We kept a big wine-making barrel in the basement of the Big House. When it came time to make wine, we would throw grapes in the barrel, get in barefoot, and smash the grapes. Sometimes there would be as many as four or five of us crushing grapes at the same time. We did it for hours. I sometimes had an almost uncontrollable curiosity to find out if the adults would be able to taste a difference if I peed in it, but there were always far too many people around to carry out my plans. After hours and hours of pressing, the wine was left to sit for weeks. At the end of this process, they would drain the wine. What remained of the pulp would be run through a still and transformed into the strongest, smelliest moonshine you can imagine. It was so strong that it usually had to be diluted into coffee or used to can cherries. I could never understand why, when the family drove out to a picnic—we went to the Green River Gorge most often—we brought coffee cups instead of glasses. The men used to play bocce, a form of lawn bowling called "boules" in France. They would put wine in the coffee cups so that no one would know that there was alcohol on the premises. Only later did I understand the crucial importance of the coffee cups.

CHAPTER ONE

We made a dark wine from Zinfandel grapes, and only drank it during meals. I can never remember any clan members drinking wine between meals. The children could drink wine with their meals if they wanted to, but to this day I can't drink wine because I still remember the terrible sour smell of the family wine.

Holiday dinners at the Big House were such large affairs that they demanded two dining rooms, one for adults and one for kids. My grandfather, my godfather and my four great uncles would always show up with their own individual bottles of family wine. The one common feature these wines shared were their bottles, which were all dark brown and corked in the same way.

Each of the men made his wine differently, custom-produced to please his particular taste. Some would use only zinfandel grapes, others would add sugar, others added muscatel grapes and still others made pure muscatel wine. The men would position the bottles on the table directly across from their own place setting. Looking at the bottles standing tall on the table, and watching the smiles of pride directed at them by the men, I would always think to myself, "If they somehow drank out of the wrong bottle, they couldn't tell the slightest difference between the various flavors." It was typical of me that I wanted to find a way to infiltrate the dining room and, unbeknownst to the men, switch their bottles around.

During one holiday celebration, I got lucky. For a few minutes the dining room stood empty at the same time that the uncorked, nearly identical wine bottles stood tall on the table. I seized my opportunity and switched the bottles every which way.

Once dinner started, I could hear enraged voices from the main dining room complaining about bad wine and shouting about treachery. Lo and behold, those Italians did know a thing or two about wine! Everyone accused everyone else of playing a dirty trick. I didn't say a word but just sat there looking down at my plate, praying that I might somehow escape discovery.

Finally, though, after much display of passion on the part of the adults, a little six-year-old cousin I obviously hadn't noticed while committing my crime blew the whistle on me. I was forced to take drastic measures of self-protection. I ran behind my grandmother. No one, not even Ernesto, would have dared challenge Grandmother in this situation. The men called me every Italian name in the book. This was serious business. If you learned one thing quickly about Italians, it was to stay away from their women and their wine, but not necessarily in that order.

Looking back, I can see there were just too many ways to beat Prohibition, and people didn't have to think very hard to do it. One day, the police raided the stucco house I lived in with my grandparents. Who knew who had informed on us? Obviously it wasn't one of our clan, because that would have endangered them as well. And why in the world would they want to, anyway? The police probably targeted us as likely wine-drinking

CHAPTER ONE

candidates because we were Italian. And if this was their reasoning, they couldn't have been more right. I don't know an Italian who doesn't enjoy a glass of red wine at least now and again. I knew that the wine was kept in bottles under the sink, but when the half-dozen or so police stormed the house, they looked everywhere—the basement, the closets, the back porch, the front porch, the yard—everywhere, that is, except for under the sink. They left, completely cowed, beneath the disapproving gaze of my grandmother. Even at my tender age, I couldn't believe their incompetence. "How dumb can they be?" I asked myself.

More Mischief

Even though I never got the chance to pee in the family wine, I was able to work my mischief in other ways. One of the best occasions for this was shortly after the Fourth of July, when everyone was lulled into a false sense of security. On the Fourth, Uncle Fred proved himself a patriot by always bringing along a collection of enormous firecrackers. In hindsight, after flying as a tail gunner on a B-24, I can see today that those firecrackers were pretty damn dangerous.

I guess Uncle Fred wasn't overly concerned about child safety, though, because he always gave me some of those miniature sticks of dynamite—and then I would steal a few more. These fireworks I would use strategically over the next few days. The best day was Sunday. Everyone worked hard on the farm all week and Sunday

39

afternoon was their time for napping in rocking chairs. I would wait until three or four of the men were asleep and then quietly set up a firecracker under each chair. Lighting the fuses consecutively, I wouldn't run away. Instead, I preferred to stay and watch the damage I had wrought. When they jumped out of their chairs, you would have thought they were not long from a combined quadruple heart attack. None of them ever had one, though. When they saw me howling behind their chairs, I had to run for my life. I made a beeline for a cherry tree on the west side of Grandma's house. Once there, I clambered up the tree and onto the roof. I would hear angry voices, often swearing in Italian dialect, calling for my head. I laid low on the roof, waiting for the voices to calm down, but laughing like a madman on the inside. Only Grandmother knew my hiding place, but I knew she would never give me away. I was Grandma's favorite, and she was mine. Of course my grandmother never knew everything I did to the clan's men. If she had, I might have felt a lot less secure on that roof.

Grandmother wasn't always the safest person to be around, that's for sure. Grandmother's oldest son was my Uncle Fred. I loved having him around because he was so funny. Once in a while he would have a few too many drinks and he would be even funnier, but it was then that he swore a lot. Boy, could he let some choice language roll off of his well-oiled tongue!

One day Uncle Fred's influence made itself felt on me in a painful way. I was trying to build a model airplane out of two small pieces of wood. As I swung down to hit the nail, I missed, absolutely shattering one of the pieces of wood. As my airplane disintegrated in front of my eyes, I started swearing like crazy, using some of Uncle Fred's best bad language. My grandmother, with her ever-sharp ears, heard me. As a punishment, she tied me to a tree trunk. I was hollering and swearing even louder now, and Grandmother took advantage of my poor judgment by somehow managing to shove a bar of soap into my mouth. Stupidly, this didn't stop me from screaming and, biting into the soap, I suddenly had soap all over my mouth, in between my teeth and on my tongue. It tasted awful.

I really don't know how long I was tied to the tree trunk—it couldn't have been much more than an hour, if that—but at what I guess must have been around 5:00 p.m. (the usual dinner time), Grandmother finally untied me and told me to prepare for dinner. Still madder than an unhappy hornet, I slinked downstairs and spotted a can of white paint. Paint was so primitive in those days that it took it a couple of days to dry properly. Intrigued by the possibilities the paint offered, I stirred the can and found a brush. With paint can and brush in hand, I sneaked back upstairs and proceeded to paint the wood toilet seat white.

That night my aunt Mary, a very attractive, sophisticated young lady, joined us for dinner. She was married to my uncle Al, Grandma's youngest son. Upon her arrival, I forgot all about being angry at Grandmother and painting the toilet seat. After dinner, I was sweeping the kitchen floor when Aunt Mary visited the upstairs bathroom. She wasn't there for long. Coming back down she looked at grandmother strangely. "Ma, why didn't you tell me that you had painted the toilet seat white?" Without a second's delay, my grandmother's and my eyes met. I dropped the clean-up broom and streaked out the back door, just ahead of my grandmother who trailed close behind with the broom in her hand, ready to do some damage to her favorite grandchild. I barely escaped. After prowling the neighborhood for about half an hour, I tried to sneak back into the house, thinking myself safe for the moment, when suddenly—POW! I was whacked across the back with a stick that grandmother always kept ready behind the stove in case just such an occasion presented itself. Afterwards, peace and quiet returned to the house, but I can guarantee you that no one sat on the toilet seat for a few days. Fortunately, Grandmother wasn't one to hold grudges, at least not toward me.

The Boss

The only clan member who could possibly presume to tell grandmother what to do was Ernesto, who lived in the big house and was the patriarch of the family. No one called him Ernesto—they just called him "Boss." And that's exactly what he was, gruffly bossing everyone around with his imperious airs. He was like something out of "The Godfather," but with no Mafia connections.

CHAPTER ONE

The Boss stood straight and tall with his enormous handlebar mustache standing out prominently on his face. He used a heated curling iron to keep it curled. He was a large man with a powerful voice. Even though he actually performed physical labor on the family farm, he was always neat and clean. He walked briskly along everywhere he went, always in command of any situation he entered into.

Whatever Ernesto said was true, even if he told a damn lie. I resented this terribly because I considered Grandma to be the boss of me, not Ernesto. As a result of my absolute devotion to my grandmother, I delighted in doing anything I could to irritate or displease Ernesto, and boy did I do a lot.

To give some sense of this, I should tell the story of my cousin, Philly Roppo. Philly had a paper route. When it came time to collect payments around the neighborhood, he would ask me, of all people, to go to the Big House and collect Ernesto's payment. I don't know if he thought I was crazy or stupid enough to do it, but when it came to Ernesto, I had more guts than I should have had. Ernesto used to fall asleep at his desk a lot, and I would stay outside his office, waiting for him to doze off. Gently walking across the office floor, I pushed his shoulder hard and asked for Philly's newspaper money.

If this weren't enough, I would also move Ernesto's spittoon, so that sometimes he would wake up and spit into emptiness on the floor. Other times I would wait for him to fall asleep and then rush home to the telephone. I can still remember the Big House's number, Kenwood 1943. There weren't phones in every room in that era, and the phone in the Big House was in the hall about eighty feet from Ernesto's office. I would alter my voice, asking "Is Ernesto there?" When he came to the phone, all he'd get was the dial tone.

Another trick I played on Ernesto happened around planting time one year. Everyone in the family helped with this part of the farm work—there was such a strong family bond in those early days that they wouldn't have dreamed of not showing up. Planting by hand was hard work and took an extremely long time. You had to make a hole in the ground for each baby plant and then pat the dirt back firm against it. One day when the family was planting lettuce next to the barn, I dug a large hole out of view on the other side and covered it with branches. I walked back around the barn and, after picking up some dry horse manure, I began to toss pieces of it at Ernesto. He got so mad that he began to chase me around the barn. I ran wide around it but Ernesto, thinking he had a good chance to cut me off, didn't run quite so wide. He regretted it. A second later, WHOOSH! Right into the hole Ernesto fell, just like a Burmese tiger trapped by hunters. What a hunting trophy Ernesto, the grand patriarch, would have made. As soon as he fell in the hole I made a beeline for Grandmother. She kept me in hiding for days while Ernesto stewed about being fooled by the likes of me.

CHAPTER ONE

Losing My Security

My grandmother had mentioned to me more than once that if she were to die, I would have a tough time of it. Truer words were never spoken. Not only would there be no one there to protect me from Ernesto, but, much more fundamentally, no one would be there to take care of me, period. As far as I was concerned, my parents, who lived about a mile away from us, were out of the question to live with. I knew that my brother, Bob, and my mother wouldn't have been so bad, but my father was a strange and terrible man. Grandmother was so vigorous and imposing it was hard to imagine her dying for a long time to come. Yet grandmother's death did come, sooner than expected and without any forewarning.

On September 6, 1936, my grandmother had a heart attack. She was only fifty-four. Cousin Georgie was staying with us because her husband, Phil, was working an out-of-town construction job at the time. When Grandmother started experiencing terrible pain, Georgie called the ambulance, which took Grandmother to Columbus Hospital. Georgie packed up all of my clothes and most of my belongings and sent me off to live with my parents. As you can imagine, I was absolutely heartbroken.

On September 7, my mother informed me that Grandma was in an oxygen tent. That scared me a lot because it sounded so drastic and I was convinced that she must be really sick for the hospital to take such extreme measures. Early the next day, I received a phone call informing me that Grandmother desperately wanted to see me as soon as possible. I was so happy because I figured that for her to want to see me must mean that she was feeling better and maybe even thinking about her return home. Nothing would have possibly pleased me more. Bob and I ran up to 65th Street to catch a bus, which took us to the University District. From there we took a streetcar to downtown Seattle, before finally jumping on a cable car that transported us to Columbus Hospital on Madison and Boren.

I remember so vividly dashing into the hospital room and seeing Grandmother's body lying there, motionless. My cousin Josephine said simply and bluntly, "Your grandmother is dead." I was devastated. For a while I stood there in shock. Then, reflexively, I drew my right hand to my lips and nudged Bob. He did the same, and both of us blew her a kiss. Bob loved Grandma just about as much as I did. The only difference between us had been that I had lived with Grandma from babyhood on. The only thing I can remember about the rest of that day was Uncle Fred walking around talking about my father: "That son of a bitch killed my mother." I didn't understand it at the time, but that was before I lived with my father while in my teens.

When Grandma died, my grandfather was very quiet and sad, but I never saw him cry. He was stoic, instead. He kept working on the farm until the end of his days. Remarrying was out of the question. Once married to Grandmother, always married to her. From then on, he spent a lot of time in his room reading the Bible, no doubt searching for solace in its pages. Grandmother had always dominated our household. Grandfather was kind and easy going, but when Grandma died, he faded into the shadows of the family even more than he had done before.

The following day was the opening session of school and I had to be there. Even though I didn't look forward to the academic side of school, the first day of school was usually a happy time because I was reunited with all of my friends I didn't see in the summer. Although I was heartbroken about the loss of my grandmother, I tried my best to act happy and carefree, as if nothing had happened. It was nearly an impossible act, but somehow I got through the day with no major tears shed. I had good friends at school, but they weren't like family, so I didn't feel comfortable with sharing Grandmother's death with them.

The only thing I can remember about the funeral was that I didn't really see it. When we arrived at the cemetery, Ernesto told me to stay in the car. I'm not sure if this was because he was concerned that I might cause trouble at the ceremony, but trouble was the last thing on my mind. I was truly sorrowful about what had happened so unexpectedly.

No one among my friends or family ever approached me to say how bad they felt or about how sorry they were for me. I guess they thought I'd be all right at home with my mom and dad. I had been exiled from a beautiful, quiet, orderly home to a loud, angry, unruly household, where I was now the oldest of five children. I would have liked someone to talk to or a private place to go, but neither of those luxuries existed in my new house. Without Grandma around, I was alone, completely alone. For instance, if I felt like crying I wouldn't go to my mother but would rather find someplace to hide, because I didn't want anyone to see my emotional vulnerability. I wanted to live with my grandfather, to return to the place I knew best.

Even without Grandmother actually being there, the house would have exuded Grandma's wonderful personality and vitality. That would have been better for me than nothing, which is more or less what I got from living with my folks. But my aunt Murfee and her family had moved into the house to pick up the slack after Grandma's abrupt departure, and they informed me that there was no room in what had been my formal home for the previous fourteen years. I even offered to forsake my old room and sleep on a cot in the hallway. But there was just "no room at the inn."

My parents' house was located on 65th and 26th Ave. NE. This house was nothing like my grandparents' place. The ground floor was simple, with a kitchen, dining room, living room, a bathroom and two bedrooms. There were two additional bedrooms upstairs. Some of the beds had wooden crates to support the mattresses in a futile attempt to keep them level. There was a basement with a furnace, a sink, a coal bin and a garage. My mother used the sink to wash clothes.

The living room was a particular embarrassment because the walls were covered with large holes. With the apparent exception of my father, who did nothing to repair them, we were all ashamed of these holes. We would try to obscure the holes by placing chairs in front of them.

By contrast to my parents' house, my grandmother's home had been a beautiful place to live. It had a large kitchen, a neat dining room with a beautiful dining table, a large mirror and floor lamps. The living room was furnished with a long davenport with two matching chairs. There was a fireplace with a mirror above it. (In those days, mirrors were expensive; having them was a kind of status symbol. If you could afford mirrors, everyone knew that your family was pretty well off.)

My grandmother had kept her home absolutely immaculate, inside and out. The grass was always well-manicured and green. Two Royal Ann cherry trees were planted on the west side of the house. The taller of the two trees had been my means of escape from the wrath of Ernesto and the other men of the clan I had occasionally tormented.

My Father

One of the things I remember most about our house was a crucifix that hung next to the clock above the kitchen table next to the stove. For me, that image came to signify not only Christ's suffering, but all of those who suffered having to endure my father.

By far the most difficult thing about moving in with my immediate family was having to cope with my father. He was a small man, only standing about five-foot-four in height and tipping the scales at one-hundred-thirty-five pounds. His face was almost always twisted into a mean glower. I've always thanked God that I didn't look like him. Whenever I looked in the mirror I thankfully saw my mother's face rather than my father's. He was a cruel man. On one occasion we were left with no electricity for two days. I can remember my father coming home on one of those evenings and cooking himself a steak on the grill outside. Then he left and headed down to the neighborhood tavern.

On top of being a cruel man, my dad was also uneducated. As everyone who lived through it firsthand can remember, getting through the Depression was no easy business. You had to be strong, tough and willing to work. My dad, though, liked to drink and gamble too much to work very hard. He worked at a fruit stand, selling fruit and vegetables. Unfortunately, we probably didn't eat as well as his customers, because he hardly supplied the family with enough food and clothing to live on. Supporting the family was what my mother, Bob and I had to do.

My father immigrated to this country when he was only eleven years old. He arrived with his father, whose name was Edward Picardo, no relation to Ernesto Picardo. Every spring, his father would make the long journey from Italy and work on the Picardo farm in South Park. For about six years, whenever summer was over, he would take his money and head back to Italy. When my father arrived, he stayed beyond the summer, and lived with his uncle, Pasquale, who owned a vegetable farm in South Park.

In the summer of 1921, my dad's father gave my grandmother a hundred dollars because he knew his son was going to marry my grandmother's oldest daughter, Georgina. Later, when my father discovered that his father had given Grandmother a hundred dollars for their wedding, he was mad—very mad. He thought that money was supposed to be his. As a punishment, he tormented my grandmother for fifteen years until she died. On September 10, 1921, my father and mother married. With the money given by my paternal grandfather, my grandmother purchased my mother's wedding dress as well as the flowers for the church. They were married on a Saturday at Our Lady of Lourdes Parish in South Park. On the Sunday after the wedding night, there was a small reception for about forty people. My mother used to tell me how happy all the children were at the wedding because of the free ice cream, which was a rarity.

My parents didn't have an official honeymoon, and by all accounts there was no honeymoon period in their marriage either. They moved into a small house on Elm Grove Street for which they paid $15 a month in rent. The house was next door to Uncle Sabino and Aunt Annette's place, which was very near the family farm. It was a real neighborhood. Across the street from the farm was a barber shop, a fire department station, a small grocery store and a blacksmith's. I was born in the house on Elm Grove Street on July 13, 1922. The whole family was picking beans when someone came out of the house and announced that Georgina had given birth to a baby boy. I guess a new birth in an Italian-Catholic family wasn't such a big deal, because everyone just kept picking beans.

I could never understand my father. To me he was the cruelest and filthiest-mouthed man I have ever known. When my grandmother was alive and my father caught wind that we were alone in the house together, he used to come over and call us every dirty name in the book. He used to make my grandmother cry like crazy, and the only thing that kept him away from her was the threat of physical punishment from Grandmother's two sons, my uncles. God, how I wished sometimes that Uncle Fred would throttle my father.

When my father found out that I was coming to live with him and the rest of my family he just laughed, smirking, "You gotta come and live with us while your grandmother is rotting in the cemetery." He was just a mean man, and that's all there is to it. He physically abused both Bob and me. When I finally summoned the nerve to tell Ernesto how terrible—almost life-threatening—it was like to live with him, he protested in disbelief, "No one could be like that." It was very hard getting through my teenage years with my father around, but I learned to live with it, and it sure did make me a survivor. What bothered me most was that my father would call Bob and me names in front of people, whether we knew them or not. He tried to humiliate us. I can't be certain why this was so important to him but I can guess that in doing it he was really describing how he felt about himself.

But I did get back at him in one satisfying way. He had a jug of Italian wine he kept hidden in the basement coal bin. I found it one day but never told him I knew about it. When he would come home drunk and start calling me names and say terrible things about grandmother, I would stay calm and wait for him to fall asleep, as he invariably did. Then I would sneak down to the coal bin and carefully piss in his jug of wine. Dad never said good bye when I left for the service. I said "Hello," when I returned.

In the early 1960s, my father developed cancer of the tongue. By that time I no longer wished him ill but I cannot imagine a more appropriate disease for him to have suffered. The doctors cut off the cancerous part of the tongue and sewed the rest to father's cheek. Eventually, the cancer spread into his gums before finally ending up in his liver and killing him shortly thereafter. As the Bible says, "If you live by the sword, you shall die by the sword."

Mondo's Death

My Great Uncle Sabino and Great Aunt Annette had two children: a daughter by the name of Georgie, and a son by the name of Mondo. Mondo was not a physically healthy person, even when I knew him when he was only in his twenties. He had what they called at the time a "leakage of the heart." He was the only one of the men who could not work on the farm because of his health. So he became a barber and had a shop in downtown Seattle.

He was the family barber and a comic as well. More than once, he would cut Ernesto's and my grandfather's hair in interesting patterns. Without the benefit of mirrors, these men wouldn't suspect a thing. Later, after they left, they would discover that their hair was cut only on one side. All hell would break loose. I loved it when Ernesto got so mad that his face turned bright red. He called Mondo on the phone: "Get your ass over here and finish the rest of my hair!" But what the hell; no one in the family ever paid Mondo. He was my hero; I wanted to be like him.

When I was about six years old, he had talked me into sitting on a small bucket. I didn't know there was a huge firecracker under it. It blew the bucket all to hell, tore my pants and singed my butt. Grandmother had had a fit, going after Mondo with a stick. I didn't care; I still wanted to be like him.

CHAPTER ONE

At twenty-five, Mondo married a lovely Italian girl (what else?) named Mollie. One night, he and Mollie went to a Saturday night dance. In those days, there were a lot of dance halls around with the Big Band sound. They came home after the dance to the house of Mondo's parents where they lived. The house felt warm, so Mondo opened the window that night. The next morning he felt very sick. He was having trouble breathing and they rushed him to Columbus Hospital. They discovered he had pneumonia and he died three days later. He and Mollie had been married only six months. It was a great shock to his family. His mother took it very hard.

In those days, those crazy Italians would bring the body in the coffin into the house, where it stayed for three days. The year was 1933, and I was eleven years old. I was horrified to see the dead body of my cousin in the house. Italians would come to the house to visit Sabino and Annette, paying their respects. The minute someone would walk into the house, the hollering and crying would start. I thought it was terrible. But still, I'd hang around, because I didn't want to miss anything. Just when everybody finally became quiet again, suddenly more people would arrive, and the hollering would start up again.

The funeral was huge. Mondo's mother and dad wore black for one year. Some of the Italians didn't play their radios for one year. I don't know if Mondo's parents did.

I don't fear death. To me it is like walking through a door. But the pain that comes with it, I don't know. I feel I'm doing the best I can with what I've got.

Father Beglen

If Ernesto was an imposing father figure and my father was a vituperative one, then Father Beglen, the pastor of St. Catherine's, was a forceful father. I first knew Father Beglen when he was in his late forties. As his name makes clear, he was of Irish descent. What his name doesn't convey, though, is that he was a very large man with a powerful voice, and the church resonated with the echoes of his words during Mass. Every word that he uttered seemed to penetrate my entire body, and I would carry his language with me for days. It was a big deterrent to vice. In a spiritual way, Father Beglen reminded me a lot of Ernesto. Looking back, I think he was a very good priest, with a lot of presence and integrity. I might not have liked Father Beglen, but I couldn't help but respect him.

Father Beglen was an ex-newspaperman from Chicago. I suppose it was from that tough business that he learned not to take "no" for an answer, even when a "no!" was absolute and final, as it often was when my grandmother uttered the word, even to a Catholic priest. The "no" Father Beglen heard from Grandmother was about Catholic school for me. He used to come over to the house every now and again to have another shot at persuading my grandparents to send me to parochial school. I assured him I would never attend, and when he asked why not, I gave him a straight answer: "Because there aren't any girls there!"

Grandma would have liked to give her confessions to Father Beglen or any of the other priests at St. Catherine's, but they didn't understand the Italian language. Finally, a Father Carmella arrived from Italy and he was assigned to the Mount Virgin Parish near the Mount Baker district in South Seattle. When Father Carmella arrived in town, Grandmother was very relieved that she could finally give a real confession. For the life of me, I could never understand what she could possibly have done wrong. Unfortunately, I had no difficulty whatsoever remembering what I had done wrong.

At St. Catherine's, the confessional was like a very cramped, black phone booth with a small window through which to talk. It was an ominous place because it was so dark. Although the priests couldn't see me, I figured they could recognize my voice. In order to prevent being recognized, I always spoke with my hand over my mouth. And, whenever possible, I tried to stay away from Father Beglen's confessional. I liked Father Allen's confessional instead because he was kind and mild-mannered, nothing like Father Beglen. Most of the time, the confessional lines were long. I would wait in the back of the line and hope that by the time my turn came, the priest would have heard enough and I would get out of there in a hurry. The first few times I did it, it was scary; but after a while I got used to it. I never grew accustomed to Father Beglen, though.

I remember our parish as being rather small. There was no school there, only the house that Father

Beglen lived in. That house still stands today. The old church has been converted into a gym. They've built a new church now, much more beautiful than its predecessor. They have a St. Catherine's School these days with a large playing field for the children. I last attended Mass there in August of 1952 when my cousin Sam Picardo drowned at Westport while fishing, but whose body was never found. A memorial Mass was held in Sam's honor. Once in the seventies I attended a wedding there, which was a much happier occasion than my previous visit. To this day, every time I drive by the old church site, it brings back a lot of memories of Father Beglen and Grandmother.

Those Catholics who didn't attend parochial school were required to attend Catechism after Mass for about forty minutes. One Sunday my buddy, Joe Mariani, and I decided to skip Catechism and go play ball instead. I figured my chances of escape were better than Joe's, as I was the faster of the two. But perched at the top of his three-story house, Father Beglen somehow spotted just me on the road to freedom. He opened the window and cried out, "Edward Picardo, get back in there!" I was caught; I had no choice. Joe, meanwhile, was long gone.

About twenty minutes later, Father Beglen came into the church and hit me as hard as he could over the head with a Bible. Now that was the power of God's Word talking! The concussion was so hard, I might as well have been a tail gunner taking a direct hit. I slid off the seat and fell onto the floor. I looked up at him, half in disbelief, half in despair. I didn't receive any sympathy for my trouble. "Don't you ever do that again!" he shouted. And I never did. Between Father Beglen's Bible and grandmother's stick, it's a wonder I didn't grow up to be a much more devout Catholic.

When my cousin Georgie got married, Father Beglen performed the ceremony. Grandmother had raised my cousin since the death of her mother, and Georgie was like a sister to me. The wedding occurred on a Saturday morning so everyone could attend, and it was followed by a reception at our house which included brunch. Father Beglen was there, too. As usual on wedding days, Father Beglen was in a jolly mood and he made more than his fair share of trips to the wine table. He got pretty well oiled, drinking homemade red wine, which was mostly made of zinfandel grapes and was a helluva lot stronger than the wine you can buy at the store today. At one point he put his arm around my shoulders and looked down on me with his bloodshot eyes, "You're a fine boy, Eddie."

I said to myself, "Oh my God, this guy is actually human. Maybe he does like me after all...."

After Father Beglen paid me this compliment, I decided a few days later to ask him if I could be an altar boy. I knew that Philly was an altar boy and was therefore treated like a tin god around the parish and our neighborhood. I figured I might get the same treatment. When I asked Father Beglen about becoming an altar boy, he was sober, which I guess was my mistake. He looked at me for a moment with an incredulous expression on his face and then let out his familiar roar, "YOU? NEVER!" I guess there were limits to Father Beglen's humanity.

One Sunday out of the month, the children of the parish would attend Holy Communion. The Saturday prior to the service we had to go to confession in order to purify ourselves so we could properly take Christ's flesh and blood in the act of Communion. My grandmother always warned me that I would burn in hell if I lied in the confessional.

As Catholics we were taught that you might live like a saint, but if you were unlucky enough to say "Godammit!" seconds before you died, you had broken one of the Ten Commandments. In committing a mortal sin, you could be denied your heavenly reward. The prospect of this put the fear of God into Catholic children, especially kids like me who led something less than saint-like lives.

One Saturday, I got stuck with Father Beglen in the confessional. I had been taught to say, "Bless me, Father, for I have sinned. It has been one month since my last confession." I must have been about thirteen years old at the time and had begun to feel desires of the flesh. I continued, "Father, I see girls around and I'm beginning to think..." when suddenly, with a roar, I heard, "DON'T THINK! DON'T THINK! IF YOU GOTTA THINK, THINK ABOUT THE SEATTLE INDIANS!" That was the name of Seattle's Pacific Coast League baseball team at the time. And even though I was a big fan of the Indians, I couldn't stop thinking about girls.

CHAPTER ONE

The Seattle Indians

And believe me, I did love the Indians. The Indians' ballpark was located near the old Civic Auditorium, more or less where the Seattle Center and Space Needle are today. The ballpark's seats were just long wooden benches. I doubt if seating capacity exceeded more than seven or eight thousand. There was a left and center field fence, just like in big league parks, but in right field were just a lot of gooseberry bushes. If a batter could knock the ball past the right fielder and into the gooseberry bushes, it counted for a home run. As you can imagine, there were quite a few inside-the-park homers.

Light poles had been raised just to the left and right of the diamond for lighting up the field at night. I can remember Joe Carscart, the Indians' third baseman, going after foul balls between the telephone poles and catching them. If the ball hit a pole, it was out of play. There weren't any bullpens. Pitchers warmed up near the dugouts so their managers could see how "live" their arms were and talk with them. It was unusual to use more than one relief pitcher in a game. In fact, it wasn't strange at all for a manager to let a starter go the distance, even if he had thrown a lot of pitches and had been knocked around a bit. Things might have been a tad primitive back then, but baseball was a game with heart and soul. It wasn't yet a business for accountants and lawyers.

The Indians played single games from Tuesday to Saturday and then offered double-headers on Sundays. This was, of course, long before the covered Kingdome was built, and there were problems sometimes with rain; Seattle isn't the driest place in the world. Quite a few doubleheaders were played during the week as well because of rain cancellations. But at least we didn't have to worry about the Kingdome roof caving in on your head! In the late 1930s, the Indians would move into their new stadium on Rainier Avenue and become the Seattle Rainiers, after the great mountain of Washington State.

PCL teams traveled up and down the West Coast by train. There were eight teams in the league: Seattle, Portland, Sacramento, Oakland, San Francisco, Los Angeles, Hollywood, and San Diego. Now, you have to remember that there wasn't any big league baseball west of St. Louis, so the PCL was the best game in town, and if we didn't have a car, we took the streetcar down to the stadium. When we couldn't make a game, we would listen to it over the radio, often sitting in rockers on the front porch. Leo Lassen was the Indians' sports announcer, and in a close game he would always say, "Hang onto your rocking chairs."

I don't remember well any of the Seattle Indian ballplayers who went on to play in the big leagues. If any of them had gone on to distinguished careers, I think I would have remembered them. Dick "Kewpie" Barrett had a chance up there but ended back in Seattle after a short stay. Barrett was a local hero, and we liked having him back in town. When he pitched, we seldom missed it. But if we couldn't make one of his games for some reason, we invariably listened to him pitch on the radio.

The big leagues only had eight teams apiece in each league. We read about their games in the paper, but we couldn't listen to regular season games on the radio. Only the World Series was broadcast over the airwaves, and anyone who had a radio could expect people to invite themselves over for the games. I can distinctly remember listening to the games at Fairview Grade School in Mrs. Lessy's classroom. And the sports pages of the newspapers I sold detailed every single inning of every single game on the front page. When the World Series was on, it seemed as if the people of the country completely stopped their business and for a week or two became baseball fans.

The Series I remember best as a kid is the one in which the St. Louis Cardinals won the whole enchilada in 1934, a rarity in the era of Babe Ruth's and Lou Gehrig's New York Yankee dominance. The pitching Dean brothers, Dizzy and Daffy, both won two games, giving the Cards the Series. St. Louis never owed so much to one mother.

Across the street from my newspaper stand on 45th Street NE in Seattle's Wallingford district was a market. One Saturday this market had a big sale on Wheaties. You could buy a big box for ten cents. Wheaties must have been one of the sponsors for the Indians, and I can remember the jingle they used to sing over the radio: "Won't you buy Wheaties, the best breakfast food in the land?" I guess their ad campaign worked, because I still eat Wheaties today.

On this particular Saturday, a bunch of the Seattle Indians were at the store, autographing boxes of Wheaties. These were guys like the catcher Hal Spindell; pitcher Dick Barrett; infielders Billy Sheeby, Fred Muller, Chet Smith and Joe Carscart; and outfielders Bill Lawrence, Freddie Berger and Mike Hunt (who hit thirty home runs one season). Because the Indians were the only game in town, those players were like gods to my buddies and me.

When I saw the collection of Indians all in one place, I couldn't resist the temptation to leave my stand and take a closer look at them. They fulfilled all of my expectations, because they were polite and genuinely committed to pleasing their fans. They understood the connection between a community and a sports team and they were out there to solidify that connection.

When I finally returned to my stand after gaping at the players, I found the everyday people of Wallingford to be just as honest and genuine as the ballplayers. They had all left money for their papers. When I counted the papers left and the money paid I discovered that everything was accounted for.

Not so honest and genuine was the owner of the Indians. One year the owner promised the Indians' best pitcher, Dick Barrett, a $500 bonus if he won twenty games. Now, I know that doesn't sound like a lot, but five C-notes could pay for a brand new car back then. For

CHAPTER ONE

a minor leaguer it was a heap of cash. Barrett was an amazing pitcher. He's the only young pitcher I ever saw who had a pot belly and could still throw a fastball ninety miles an hour. When he let one fly, the ball just exploded into the catcher's mitt. There was no way the batter could make contact. The fans nicknamed him "Kewpie" and he was extremely popular.

On the last day of the season in which he was trying to win the $500 bonus, Barrett had already won eighteen games. There was a doubleheader scheduled that day but it seemed impossible that Barrett could win his bonus. Barrett pitched the first game and won. Now, the manager was a player's manager and he was also a crowd pleaser. Everyone in the stands wanted to see Barrett pitch for his bonus and win twenty games. So the manager handed Barrett the ball once more and told him to go out and earn his bonus. The first game had been nine innings but the second game was only scheduled for seven, so even though Barrett's arm must have been tired, he still had a reasonable chance to come through with a victory. I can tell you one thing, no spectators went home, once they saw Barrett stride out to the mound again to start the second half of the doubleheader.

Sure enough, Barrett was such a gutsy and talented player that he labored through the game for the win. Sixteen innings and two victories. Shortly after the game, the owner fired the manager for no other reason than that he had given Barrett the chance to win his bonus. The Seattle fans were outraged. I can still remember my Uncle Fred referring to the owner, using his favorite phrase, "that asshole." Uncle Fred captured well what Seattle felt about that owner. I always wondered if Barrett shared some of his bonus with the manager to help ease the pain of losing his job in the middle of the Depression.

Betty

When I wasn't gawking at baseball players at the newsstand, I was often gawking at girls. With or without Father Beglen's prohibitions against the opposite sex, I loved watching women walk by. Sometimes it made it difficult to concentrate on selling newspapers. At this point, Bob and I had a 1931 Chevrolet, so it was actually possible to act when we saw a pretty girl. We could ask her out for a date, if the opportunity arose.

One girl in particular kept catching my eye at the newspaper stand. She would walk by our corner a couple of times a week on her way to her dancing lessons in a small building half a block away. She was very pretty, five-foot-five with dark hair and a helluva lot of sex appeal. Every time she would come by, she and I would talk more and more. I found out that her name was Betty and she was seventeen—an older woman. Betty was interested in dancing and acting. She appeared in all the school plays at Lincoln High School.

As Betty and I got to know each other better, she asked me one day, "Did you ever do it?" By the way the conversation was going I knew exactly what she meant.

CHAPTER ONE

I didn't quite know what to say. Of course I had never done it! Father Beglen said you had to use self-control because if you die with a mortal sin on your soul you would go straight to hell. This was a pretty heavy burden to carry. But because I was now living with my parents, I was a member of the Assumption parish on 65th and 32nd NE. Father Beglen, meanwhile, remained at St. Catherine's, so I never had to worry about going through confession with him again. This might have been the best thing about having to move into my parents' house.

After Betty had been bold enough to ask me that question, I knew I had to take her out on a date. I asked her out to the Green Lake Theater to see a movie featuring Mae West. But my goal wasn't to take her home right after the movie. No, I had made other plans that I thought Betty might be interested in. And I wasn't disappointed.

On the farm was a large pile of empty crates we put our produce in. This box pile was near the barn, next to one of the greenhouses, which was alongside a lettuce patch. The morning before my date I went to the farm and piled those boxes in such a way that I could fit my car between the stacks and still ensure perfect invisibility from beyond the farm.

After the movie we warmed up for the feature attraction of the evening by driving and parking at Green Lake. Betty was a passionate kisser and I couldn't wait to get her alone. After a little while I told her about my place and she wanted to go see it. I was more than happy to oblige. We headed for the box pile. Upon arrival, the car fit between the crates perfectly. I was so proud.

When we got in the back seat, the first words Betty uttered were, "Are you sure you've done this before?" My damn right thumb was giving me away. It kept getting in the way every time I was about to penetrate her. Finally I succeeded. She never stopped smiling. As I look back today, I think I should have run up the small road between the lettuce and the cabbage yelling, "I'm number one! I'm number one!" Even if I wasn't number one, I felt like it.

Betty taught me to become a pretty good dancer. We went to school dances together. She enjoyed the movies and liked the musical comedies of the period the most. That's when I started to enjoy them as well. Betty talked all the time about getting into show business, and she often brought me into the act by showing me how at acting school they taught the students how to hold and kiss each other. Once this started, we always ended up on the davenport or in the bedroom. Of course we only did this when her parents were away from home, which happily for us was pretty often. Although we both knew we were headed in very different directions, we enjoyed each other, and we remained friends always. When I left for the army I told Betty that I would see her when I got back. I thought we could kick the hell out of the Japanese Empire in six months or so. How wrong I was! As it turned out, I did look for Betty again during the war. Before I went overseas and while on leave, I went to visit her. But she was away, dancing in a USO show. Boy, did I miss her.

CHAPTER TWO

Making Trouble in High School

Roosevelt High School

Odd Jobs

When I went to live with my parents after my grandmother died, the Depression was in full swing. Economic troubles plagued not just my family but the whole country as well. My brother Bob and I became very close, seeking out odd jobs to help support the family.

The odd job I hated most was shoveling sawdust into the basement of houses to be used as fuel for sawdust burners. In those days, homes were heated primarily with sawdust burners. The sawdust would get in our eyes and ears, up our noses and down our backs. It drove me crazy! On top of that, it was also very hard work. Sometimes Bob and I would get yard work instead, which I didn't mind much. It was easy, compared to shoveling sawdust.

In order to avoid the pains of sawdust shoveling, I got a morning paper route with the *Post Intelligencer* (in Seattle we call it the *"P.I."*) in the Ravenna district of Seattle. Bob got a paper stand on the corner of 45th and Meridian, a busy thoroughfare which promised to be a profitable spot for the Picardo brothers. Also on this corner was a bakery, Korka's, owned by a nice old German couple. The Korkas were childless. Once in a while I would help Bob out selling papers. The Korkas got to know Bob and me. They liked the fact that we showed a lot of spirit.

Like most shops in the 1930s, Korka's was closed on Sundays. The couple approached me one day and asked if I would be willing to scrub down their bakery on Sundays. They offered me two dollars for about four to five hours worth of work, which in 1936-37 was big money for a kid. I grabbed at the chance. So between the paper corner, the paper route and the bakery, Bob and I were doing pretty well. Bob made sure that most of our earnings went to Ma. Sometimes I would have liked to splurge, but Bob would stop me from spending my money on foolish things. We knew we couldn't rely on our dad for much of anything. We had to be the men of the family and bring home the bacon.

I can remember that the death of almost any movie star would instantly sell papers. When the Hindenberg burned, that sold a lot of papers as well. And believe me, Hitler and Mussolini sold papers, too. In 1938, when Hitler occupied Czechoslovakia against the wishes of England and France, the headline simply read, "WAR." As it turned out, of course, Neville Chamberlain would return from a negotiated settlement with Hitler, proclaiming that England had won "peace with honor." Only later would we learn how wrong old Chamberlain was. But when that headline came out, I knew I had to do something to capitalize on it. So I climbed up a telephone pole as high as I could go and nailed the paper to it. We sold a helluva lot of papers that day. On Sunday mornings Bob would sell papers (which were a dime at that time), and I would scrub the bakery.

One week Bob and I made a whopping eighteen dollars selling papers. A man who worked at Ernst, a hardware store in Seattle, heard about it. He asked us how it was possible. He only made $12.50 a week. I asked him how much his manager made. He said $25.00. I suggested, "You need to work hard to become a manager, and then two teenagers selling papers down the street won't be earning more than you!"

A certain pickup truck used to come by every weekday. The passengers would buy two copies of the *Seattle Times* and a *Star*, which amounted to an eight cent sale. The *Times* was three cents each, and the *Star* was two cents. For months that was always our biggest sale of the day. It was like money in the bank. One day when I was selling papers on the corner, they came by. I rushed over immediately and handed them their three papers. The guy said, "I'll pay you tomorrow, kid." I never saw him again. I had been suckered. I learned a good lesson that day that I haven't forgotten to this day. No promises, please, just let me see the money.

If it hadn't been for selling newspapers on 45th and Meridian, I might still be in agony with a terrible toothache. I went to the family dentist, Dr. Crowley, to have him pull it out. After looking the tooth over, Dr. Crowley said matter of factly, "It will cost you two dollars." I replied just as matter of factly that I didn't have two dollars to my name. He told me, "Well, when you get two dollars, come back and I'll pull out the offending tooth." You can better believe that I worked my tail off for the next two weeks to reach the two century mark in profits.

My Role Model

During the Depression Bob and I were always on the lookout for bargains. One time during the summer we were at J.C. Penney's in the University District. We had about fifty cents between us, and there was a big table loaded with swimsuits at thirty-nine cents each. Being the oldest brother, I told Bob to get a suit for himself. He objected, "No, you."

I told him, "No, you." We went round and round like this before Bob, apparently surrendering, finally agreed to take the fifty cents. In the meantime, I kept looking around the store for more bargains. All of a

CHAPTER TWO

sudden, Bob threw a paper bag at me. "Here's your swim suit." We were the same size, so I said, "No, Bob, you take it." He refused, but when we got outside he smiled proudly, "Eddie, I'm wearing mine already."

When Bob and I both were attending Roosevelt High School, I was sixteen months older and one grade ahead of him. But these differences didn't amount to much. We were best friends and resembled each other so much that we could have been twins.

After school one day, we spotted a motorcycle. It was very large with wide handle bars. Bob somehow got the damn thing started and began driving it around the main floor of the school. After he made a few revolutions he brought it back to where he found it and parked it, just like nothing had happened.

The next morning at about five minutes to nine, just before classes started, the phone rang in the classroom. The teacher listened for a minute, hung up and then turned to me. "You're wanted in the principal's office." I couldn't for the life of me understand why the principal would want to see me. But it wasn't a request, it was an order, and I couldn't very well turn him down. I kept thinking to myself, "If I've done something wrong, I would know it, wouldn't I?"

When I walked into the principal's office, he started right in on me, as if I had committed a murder. He told me that I had been spotted on a motorcycle on the main floor. Doing these kinds of things, he warned, signaled that I was going to turn out to be a rotten person. I was instructed to get a note from my mother promising that I would never behave in such a way again. (As if there would be a motorcycle waiting every day for Bob and me!) I just nodded about everything he demanded. As I opened the door and headed out of his office, he wrapped things up with, "Eddie, why don't you try to be more like your brother, Bob?" If only the principal knew! I was dying with laughter inside. I never told Bob who the principal had suggested to me as a role model. Maybe if I wanted to go into the motorcycle or swimsuit business, Bob would have been a good role model at the time.

Only once did I really get burned up at the principal. He accused me of taking a bunch of high school kids into a garage near the school and teaching them how to smoke. Me?! Teach someone how to smoke? He had to be kidding. This I never did. I did not smoke then nor at any time during my life, as my pilot, Edgar Spencer, the man who bummed my seven packs of cigarettes off me, would gladly corroborate if he's still alive. I have my doubts about Edgar being alive, though, because he smoked like a chimney. We didn't know how bad smoking was during the war, but we sure do now. I don't think Edgar would have lived to a ripe old age. Who knows, though? He was a survivor, that's for sure.

Although I never taught anyone how to smoke, I was always up to something all through high school. My good buddy, Joe Mariani, and I took a cooking class together. One day we had to cook something in our oven. We had small tin gas stoves set up next to each other in two rows of ten. For some reason the teacher was out of the room and Joe turned on the gas to light the oven. He turned to me and asked, "Do you have a match?" "No," I replied. "Well, we're going to need one to light the oven." I said, "That's right, Joe, why don't you go find one?"

When Joe left in search of matches, he forgot to turn off the gas. During Joe's absence, we could start to smell the fumes, which emptied the classroom except for me. Joe returned with a match and got ready to light the stove. For some reason I stuck around to see what would happen. As the lighted match got nearer to the oven I said to myself, "This is going to be good." BANG! The explosion literally blew off the oven door and singed Joe's hair, eyebrows, nose and face. In seconds, the teacher was back in the room, hollering, "What happened?!" She looked at Joe and asked if he was all right. As it turned out, Joe and I were okay, but we got kicked out of the class, pronto.

The Bachelors Club

Four of us at Roosevelt High formed a club that we called the *Bachelors Club*. Joe was the President, I was the Vice-President, Buddy was the Treasurer and Jim Casey was the Secretary. We never let anyone else join the club simply because no one wanted to.

One day I was running late for school and, without noticing it, I showed up at school wearing my pajama top. Nobody really noticed, not even the teachers. But the guys in the club sure noticed. The next day, all four of us showed up at school wearing our pajama tops. And on the following day, about eighty students showed up in pajama tops. Mr. Gridley, the principal, had a fit.

The phone rang in class and the teacher turned and looked at me. "Eddie, you are wanted in the principal's office."

I told her, "Okay, but I'm sick and tired of hearing, 'Eddie, you are wanted in the principal's office.' I'm changing my name to Sam!"

When I walked into Mr. Gridley's office, he said, "Eddie, you are causing disreputable behavior. This idea of starting a trend with pajama tops is unacceptable. Anyone coming to school tomorrow wearing them will be expelled, and a notice will be in every class within the hour."

"Sir," I said, "I would like to change my name to Sam."

"What are you talking about?" he asked. "Now get out of here, and start acting like a normal human being." Boy, he sure was asking for a lot. But the next day, not one pajama top was seen.

Not long after that, all four of us walked over to the Picardo Farm. We went in the barn and found a bunch of dirty overalls. We grabbed them, put them on—though they didn't fit very well—and headed for Skid Row in downtown Seattle, which centered around First and Main. My teacher, Miss Farrell, had said I was going to end up as a dishwasher on Skid Row. I wanted to know what my future environment might be like.

CHAPTER TWO

In high school I already had a dark beard, so I looked older than the rest of the guys. A guy on Skid Row saw me standing around and asked me for a drink. I told him I didn't have one. He pulled out a pint of apple jack wine and said, "Here, have one on me."

"No, thanks," I said, and we walked away. On First and Cherry, there was a man selling jumbo hot dogs on a bun, with relish and mustard, for only ten cents each. Boy, were they good—and they filled us up, too.

Down the street was a secondhand store. We walked in and spotted a bunch of black derby hats made of cardboard for ten cents each. We bought four of them. You guessed it. The next morning, the members of the Bachelors Club all showed up with black derbies. We were a big hit. Everyone at school asked, "Where did you get those?" Lots of kids wanted one, too.

We told them to go to University Book Store: "There's lots of them!" The next day, of course, we were still the only ones with black derbies, because they weren't in the Book Store at all. When Mr. Gridley saw us with our new hats, all he said when he saw me was, "You look good in yours, Sam." We were a force to be reckoned with!

Pork Chop Lips

When we attended Roosevelt High School, there was a music teacher by the name of Mr. Worth. He was head of the school band and was after me constantly to play the tuba. "With your lips," he told me, "you would make an excellent tuba player."

I wanted no part of playing the tuba. I thought it was too ugly and too heavy to carry around. He said, "I could also teach you to play the bass fiddle." That was also too big to carry around. He said, "You could play at the school dances, the assemblies, even some of the sporting events." He wouldn't give up. Whenever I'd see him coming down the hall, I would turn around and go the other direction.

One day I asked him what was so special about my lips. He referred to them as "pork chop lips," perfect for playing the tuba.

That did it. I gave him a firm, "NO!" As I look back, though, I regret not learning to play the tuba and bass fiddle. It would have been fun to play the bass in a band today.

When Joe Mariani found out that Mr. Worth had liked my "pork chop lips," Joe nicknamed me that, laughing when I told him to stop. Sometimes he would say, "Okay, I won't call you that...Liver Lips!" I told him if he ever called me that in front of a girl, I would throw him off the school roof.

Bob Eckberg, Sam Glass and Me

Besides Joe, I had another close friend, a kid by the name of Bob Eckberg. We had some classes together, which looking back on it was bad news for most of our teachers. We both slept a lot in class, though I always thought I had a legitimate excuse because my morning

P.I. route forced me out of bed by five o'clock. Maybe Bob was just lazy.

The first day of classes one semester, Bob and I had to register for an English composition class. We wanted to sign up with a teacher by the name of Sam Glass. Everyone really liked Mr. Glass. Whenever we would see him in the hall or lunchroom, we always went up to talk to him. This was different from most of the other teachers whom we avoided like the plague. The reason we loved Mr. Glass was that, unlike his peers, he listened to his students. When Bob and I approached the registration table to sign up for Mr. Glass' class, he took one look at us and said, "Oh no, not you two." But we begged him. We knew we didn't want any other teacher but him.

After a long debate, and with a long line of kids forming behind us, he finally agreed to take us on, but only under certain clear conditions. We were told to sit in the back of the class and not bother any of the other students. And we had to keep our mouths shut for the entire semester. He declared, "I can't teach you two anything, but I'm not worried about it. Both of you will get your education outside of the classroom. Keep your ears open; maybe you'll learn something useful. If you do as I say, I will give both of you a C for good behavior." Good old Mr. Glass! Sounded like a damn good deal to me.

So Bob and I followed instructions. We sat in the back of the class every day and didn't bother anyone. One day Mr. Glass asked me a question and I said, "Sam, you know I don't know the answer Why embarrass me in front of the class?"

He said, "Oh, I'm sorry Mr. Picardo."

At that point Bob spoke up and complained, "Hey, Sam, you woke me up."

He apologized, "Sorry, Mr. Eckberg." From then on, the names stuck. To us he was "Sam" and we were "Mr. Picardo" and "Mr. Eckberg." You may say today that we didn't respect him, but we did in our own way, very much. When given the chance, after class we would talk to him about our ups and downs, which were many.

In the summer months Sam used to head over to Whidbey Island where the government was building its military base. He said he dug ditches there for eight dollars a day to make ends meet. He was a hard worker. Just after the bombing of Pearl Harbor, Bob and I stopped by to tell him that we were going to enter the service. I told him I was going to join the Air Force and Bob told him he was planning to be a Navy pilot. You had to be pretty darn good to catch on as a Navy pilot. Sam just shook his head in amused wonder. "Bob, you'll never make it. You'll fall asleep trying to land the plane on the carrier." I totally agreed with Sam. But to prove our teacher wrong, Bob laid down a five dollar bet that he would succeed as a Navy pilot.

Unbelievably, Bob did indeed join the Navy, became a pilot, and never once fell asleep trying to land on a carrier. He was even decorated three times and was shot down over Tokyo Bay, where he was eventually picked up by a U.S. submarine. All that adventure and danger yet Bob could only talk about how great the food was on the submarine. What a guy.

After the war, Bob Eckberg and I went back to our old Roosevelt High stomping grounds so Bob could collect the five bucks he had coming to him. Old Sam was sure glad to see us. I thought maybe I saw a few tears in his eyes, but maybe he only had a cold. Sam said he was proud of us. "I heard that between the two of you guys you were decorated eight times," he said. "I knew you two could do it." Then I started to explain that we both had received the Good Conduct Medal. He stopped me in mid-sentence, "That I'll never believe." "Sam," I said, "We were given the Good Conduct Medal. I never said we earned it." Sam laughed, "That, I'm willing to believe." Sam was terrific. We always left him feeling better about ourselves than we had before we spoke with him.

In the years following World War II, I read somewhere that Sam was very instrumental in getting teachers more assistance, more benefits and enough money so they didn't have to dig ditches in the summer. And by the way, Bob and I both got a C in his class. We might not have been the best composition students in the world, but we knew how to keep up our half of a bargain. We never bothered a soul in that class, except maybe for Sam a few times. But even so, I'm pretty sure he was sorry to see us go.

Rumors of War

Shortly after I joined the U.S. Army Air Force, I received a letter from my brother, informing me that he had been turned down as a pilot by the U.S. Army Air Cadet program because he was color-blind. Then he wrote and told me that he had tried to join the Seabees (Navy Construction) but had been turned down by them as well.

Finally, I received a letter from Bob which explained that he had been classified as 4-F and disqualified from military service. Seems he had what the military called at the time "stomach nervousness." I could hardly believe that Bob Picardo wasn't good enough for the military. In school he had been the best athlete of us all. As a freshman he was a first string catcher on the Roosevelt varsity baseball squad. He was a long ball hitter with a powerful throwing arm. How could he possibly have been 4-F? During the war Bob went down to Oakland, California, to work for Uncle Fred in a joint called the Midway Bar. Bob's Midway turned out to be a heckuva lot safer than the Midway those sailors fought at in the Pacific.

Joining the Army Air Force wasn't my first experience with the military. In November of 1937, when I was still only fifteen, I joined the Washington National Guard. We were supposed to be eighteen to join, but I felt like I was ready. We would drill one night a week at the Old Armory on Western Avenue downtown, just north of Pike Place Market.

CHAPTER TWO

The main reason I joined was because every three months we received a check for twelve dollars, which came in mighty handy. Bob always made sure that Ma got some of it, which was okay with me. In the summer the National Guard would spend two weeks at Camp Murray, near Fort Lewis, and we would get paid extra for that, too. I was assigned to "C" Battery of the 146th Field Artillery of the Rainbow Division of the U.S. Army. I became a gunner corporal on an old French 75 millimeter artillery gun.

In 1940, as war raged throughout Europe and Asia, President Roosevelt declared a national emergency. He and his advisors knew that the U.S. could be drawn into the war at any time and needed to be prepared for it. Men over eighteen had to be drafted and serve one year in the military. Some of the National Guard units around the country were called up for active duty, including the Rainbow Division. This was effective as of September 16, 1940. Telegrams were sent out to my unit for guardsmen to report for active duty. Mysteriously, I never received a telegram, even though I had more than two months of my enlistment to serve. I didn't push it, though. I was in no great hurry to enter into active duty. After all, I was still a kid in high school.

One day, while I was daydreaming, looking out the window at school, I saw an Army truck stop in front of the building. Not conceiving that an Army truck could have anything to do with me, I didn't think much of it. Shortly after the truck stopped, our classroom phone rang.

The teacher answered it, then turned and looked toward me. "Eddie, you're wanted in the principal's office." What now? I hadn't been riding motorcycles or teaching anyone how to smoke. What could the rap possibly be today?

After a slow walk down the halls of Roosevelt High School, I finally reached the principal's office. The principal said simply, "Eddie, you were sent a telegram."

"No," I said. "I never received a telegram." But no one believed me. The soldiers who had been sent to retrieve me took me down to the armory, where the Seattle Center is located today. They took me to see a captain who asked me why I had failed to report. It wasn't until 1993 that my mother finally told me the truth. She had received a telegram and had never shown it to me. She didn't want me to go off to war.

I served with the guards at Camp Murray and later at Fort Lewis. I went to night school at Clover Park High to finish my degree. Luckily, the government sponsored this program. In November I could have gotten out of the Guard because my enlistment ended then. Once out of the Guard I would have had to register and wait to be drafted in order to put in my one year of active service. So instead of leaving the Guard, I signed up again in order to put in my one year of active duty and not worry about being drafted.

I remember the summer of 1941 very well. It looked like the U.S. might avoid war after all. We Guardsmen drove in trucks through Oregon and down into California. It was the first time in my life that I had left the state of Washington and I absolutely loved it. We practiced war games in California. In June we heard that Germany had invaded Russia. I bet a guy five dollars that the Germans would never reach Moscow. It turned out I was right but I never collected that bet. My friend was killed later in the South Pacific.

November finally arrived and I was excited because I had done my duty. Finally discharged, I was looking forward to civilian life. And then two weeks later the Japanese bombed the hell out of Pearl Harbor. Suddenly, after the U.S. declaration of war against Japan, I was back to Square One. In a single morning, the Japanese Navy had altered my life forever. Maybe my life wouldn't last much longer, but I knew one thing: If I was going to exit this world I was going to go down kicking and screaming. My career as a tail gunner was just around the corner.

The War Begins

On Sunday, December 7, 1941, I was working part-time during the Christmas season at MacDougal's Department Store in downtown Seattle. I don't know why, but for some reason they stuck me in the Chinaware Department. I was clumsy as an ox, but I still somehow managed to put up the china displays without breaking a thing. Stores were closed on Sundays in those days, so I worked alone during the day, once I had received instructions from my supervisor.

When we knocked off for the day, I walked out of the door on Second and Pike. A man walked by, swearing, "Those damn Japs!" Someone else walked by, and I asked him what had happened. He said the Japanese had bombed Pearl Harbor. It had been a sneak attack while the Japanese ambassadors were talking peace in Washington, DC. I was absolutely infuriated.

I went to a gasoline station not far from my home, near the east end of Green Lake where my friends and I used to hang out. A lot of guys were already there talking about what had happened. I had been thinking hard on my way over, and I told them I wanted to join the Air Force. Joe Mariani, a kid I grew up with, said he was going to join the Navy and that they had an Air Force. He suggested that we join together. Knowing Joe too well, I told him that when the shooting started I wanted to be as far away from him as possible. My brother, Bob, used to refer to Joe and me as the Laurel and Hardy of Roosevelt High School. We were always in some kind of trouble. What we didn't realize was that two of our closest high school buddies, Jim Casey and Bud Libby, had quit school to join the Navy. They had both been on the *U.S.S. Arizona*. Fortune had smiled on Bud Libby. He had been transferred off the *Arizona*, but Jim Casey was still on it, and he's entombed there today.

About three days after the bombing of Pearl Harbor, I read in the paper that General Tojo, Japan's Prime Minister had announced, "We will enslave the United States of America, and I will give the order from the White House steps."

CHAPTER TWO

"Ya!" I said when I read it. "Well, it will have to be over my dead body!"

The thing about the Japanese attack on Pearl Harbor is that it brought the country together. It was probably the last time that American unity was so complete. When I stopped by the Army Service Center to get information about joining up, I ran into an old high school history teacher of mine. Her name was Miss Wiley and she had been my history teacher in 1939. I liked her pretty well as a teacher, and I think she was one of the few teachers who liked me. She was a large, pleasant-looking woman and she seemed to be a happy person because she smiled a lot.

When I met Miss Wiley at the Service Center she seemed very happy to see me. She talked about the war and told me, "I hate to see so many young men going off to fight a war." I agreed. "But we really don't have a choice, do we?" I said. Joining the U.S. Army Air Force took some time. I had to fill out a long questionnaire and take a number of tests, as well as pass a physical. Somehow I came out smelling like a rose. I often wondered if Miss Wiley had something to do with it, because she helped correct the test papers.

When I left she wished me well and said, "I hope to see you again." She probably thought I would never return alive.

One morning a bunch of Army recruits and I climbed into a truck on Fourth and Jackson in downtown Seattle. A smart-ass sergeant stood behind the truck while we sat in the back end. He smirked, "Don't worry about anything, boys. You're all leaving Seattle as heroes. You don't have to come back."

I told him, "That's okay, we'll do your fighting for you." The sergeant gave me a dirty look, and I shot one back at him, too. He just turned and walked away like a ruptured duck. I hope my statement made him think twice about what he said. One thing I knew was that he couldn't do a thing to punish me because I hadn't been sworn in yet. At Fort Lewis we took some more tests and were sworn in. I wouldn't be able to respond to my superiors so flippantly again.

Las Vegas, New Mexico

After Fort Lewis I was shipped to Las Vegas, New Mexico, a small town near Santa Fe, for three weeks of basic training, an unusually short stint. There wasn't a lot of time to spare because the war was already going strong. Our base in Las Vegas was brand new, not even fully completed. Our first week there, we stayed in tents until the barracks were ready. It was hot during the day, but at night it would get very cold. I remember a lot of marching, drilling and hearing a lecture about the army and what was expected of us as soldiers.

It was here that I first attended a USO show. I had never seen a show line on stage before. The singing and dancing were great and the comedians were extraordinarily funny. It was like something out of the real Las Vegas after the war. I really enjoyed myself—the show helped take the sting out of being in the Army.

CHAPTER TWO

Our drill sergeant was from Chicago, and we thought he must have been a gangster. His name was Marco. You guessed it: another loud and obnoxious Italian. I felt right at home. For a couple of days we practiced short order drills (marching with a rifle on your shoulder). On the third day if you made a mistake, he let you know it. I don't remember him ever talking. He only shouted. One day while he gave us a lecture, we finally found out that he was human and not an army robot. He offered us some very good advice: "Learn all that you possibly can before you go into combat. It may save you and your buddies." If he was a gangster, I'll bet he was a smart one.

At Las Vegas we also spent time in first aid classes. This was extremely helpful. I learned a lot about what to do with an injury before a medic arrived on the scene. If we listened closely, there was no question that we could save a life with our knowledge. We learned about the different kind of gas warfare we might encounter in battle. We would don our gas masks and then be placed in a tent with tear gas. They would tell you to remove your mask. I will never forget the awful taste of the gas; no one who has experienced it can ever forget. We got out of that tent in a hurry.

The three weeks in New Mexico, though hard, flew by. At the end of it, one hundred of us were shipped to Florida, where we were to attend the Embry Riddle School of Aviation, a private civilian school.

Embry Riddle School of Aviation, Coral Gables, Florida

While I was at Embry, I had read in the Police Gazette Magazine that the life of a tail gunner in combat lasted about seventeen seconds. I said, "Oh hell, I can beat that." At nineteen I was so cocky I thought I could do anything, especially if I had the chance to kick the hell out of the enemy. I wanted to attend the Aerial Gunnery School so badly I could taste it. But I was told that I had to graduate from Engineering School as a mechanic in order to qualify. I knew I had a lot of work ahead of me.

The instructors at Embry informed us that we had twelve phases to go through, with fifty-six hours for each phase. If you earned a score of below seventy in two of these courses, you were immediately sent to the 36th Street Airport in Miami and flown to North Africa to wash the sand off airplanes. I had had a less-than-successful academic record in high school, so I wanted to know why in the world I had been picked for this assignment. I figured my chances of scoring below seventy on just about any test that had to do with engineering were pretty high. They told me that my I.Q. showed that I had the ability to learn. All I knew was that I joined the Air Force to fly, not to wash sand off an airplane. I didn't intend to spend the war in some dust-ridden place like North Africa. I wanted to be in the action, not hear about it from others.

CHAPTER TWO

Embry Riddle was tough. It offered a very demanding cram course. One hundred of us were alphabetically placed into four classes of twenty-five. Four of us, Hamilton, Hanlin, La Primo and Picardo, landed in a room at the Solona Hotel, which was in Coral Gables. We later moved into the Arcade Apartments. The government was paying the tab for our housing, and if there was any left over, the school would give it to us. I wasn't holding my breath about getting extra money. But sure enough, on the first month and the months following, we would receive an envelope every month for anywhere from four to seven dollars, which in those days came in handy.

We were all proud to be members of the Embry Riddle School. It was a tradition for Embry Riddle's classes to march down the main street of Coral Gables on our way to class and sing this song:

"Oh, we're the boys from Embry Riddle you've heard so much about.

Everybody watches whenever we go out,

We're known for our wisdom and the clever things we do,

Everybody likes us, we hope you like us, too.

While we go marching and the band begins to play,

You can hear the people saying, the boys from Embry Riddle are on their way."

The citizens of Coral Gables always got a big kick out of our performance, laughing and applauding. The warm response made us feel good about ourselves. We enjoyed real unity in those days.

Being in places like Miami and Coral Gables, it was hard sometimes to stay focused on engineering. Heck, there were too many temptations around, namely women. The army was all too aware of many of the problems this posed to its soldiers. While we were stationed in Miami, we were shown a film on VD. Two fellows passed out. I got so sick I couldn't eat that day. In 1942 I don't think there was a ready cure for either syphilis or gonorrhea. So I behaved myself as well as I could in Miami, where VD was a serious problem.

The Great Roadhouse Turkey Caper

Of my roommates, Hamilton and Hanlin were carefree like me, but La Primo was initially serious and worried a lot. La Primo's seriousness didn't last long around us, however. One way La Primo broke up some of his gravity was by taking us to an Italian café about three blocks from our apartment, where you could order a large plate of spaghetti with two meatballs and French bread for only fifty-five cents. Somehow, La Primo dragged us all over there once and everyone loved it. Having eaten more than my fair share of pasta, I went for the company. I was just sick of spaghetti, but I would eat to have a chance of hanging out with my buddies.

CHAPTER TWO

One night the four of us got on a bus and went to a roadhouse that we had heard about. When we arrived there we sat at the end of the bar. The dance floor was rather large, with tables ringing it and a policeman on duty. Sitting at the end of the bar, we could see the kitchen and there, plain as day, were two cooked turkeys placed next to an open window overlooking an alley. With this scene in front of him, Hamilton got a brainstorm. He said, "Picardo, you stay here at the bar and keep an eye on the bartender. La Primo, you keep your eye on the cop. Hanlin and I will go outside. When Picardo gives us the all clear signal, I'll jump through the open window and grab the turkey."

While the policeman was talking to someone, and the bartender was busy mixing drinks, I gave my fellow conspirators the all-clear sign by grabbing my ear. Hamilton didn't hesitate. He jumped in, grabbed the turkey and threw it out the window to Hanlin. Hanlin was out of there like a shot.

Having just been an accomplice in a crime, I didn't exactly want to draw attention to myself, so I played it cool for a few minutes. A moment or two after Hamilton's turkey theft, a guy walked into the kitchen. He must have been the boss because he walked around like he owned the place. Right away he noticed that the turkey was missing—and wasn't likely to come back any time soon. His face contorted into a look of anguish and concern. He rushed out front and grabbed the bartender, asking him if he had seen anyone sneak into the kitchen.

Of course, the bartender hadn't seen any such thing. Then, noticing that I had a clear view of the kitchen, he asked me. I don't know if he was suspicious or not, but I played dumb. At this point, the boss panicked a bit and began to look all over the place for the turkey. The other employees joined in and the joint got really confused for a while. This was my opportunity. As soon as I finished my drink, I got the hell out of there as discreetly as possible.

I ran down the alley. All of a sudden Hanlin appeared, whispering, "Hey Picardo!" He tossed me the turkey like a football. As a former football player, I knew what to do with it. Unfortunately, my shirt didn't turn out as well as my hands. I had turkey grease all over my uniform and instantly became a prime suspect in the caper. We walked to the bus stop and as you can imagine, everyone was looking at me. The bus arrived and the four of us boarded without saying a word. Other passengers kept looking at us, me in particular. Finally, an older woman broke the silence and addressed me, "Young man, where did you get that cooked turkey?"

I was always a fast thinker in a pinch—I think it's part of my Italian heritage, because Italians all too often find themselves in rough situations. I told her I won it on a punch board. None of us said another word, but just kept staring straight ahead and hoping no one on that bus had just left the roadhouse. But we still felt all eyes upon us. I think even the bus driver had us in his sights in the rear view mirror! High-quality meat was in scarce supply during the war and I guess four GIs in training merited suspicion.

Every time someone would board the bus, the staring would start anew. Finally, we arrived at Coral Gables and our bus stop. We stopped at a deli, bought some beer, bread and cranberry sauce and had ourselves a feast. It might have been the best turkey I ever had. What was left, we gave away. We never went back to that roadhouse. We all had our fill of turkey.

In our apartment building lived a wealthy soldier named Roberto from New York. The only trouble with Roberto was that sometimes when he drank too much he thought he saw snakes crawling all round him. When this happened he would run up and down the hall trying desperately to escape from the snakes. The first time I heard this happening, I ran out into the hall. He grabbed me and starting begging me not to let those snakes get us. I was shocked. I had never seen or heard anything like it before. A couple of other guys and I got him off to the Army Medic, which was luckily in the same apartment building, and they eventually calmed him down so he could return to his apartment.

Two weeks later it happened again. From floor to floor, he ran through the entire apartment building. The medic retrieved him, and the Army shipped him off to a hospital in Saint Augustine in Northern Florida. We never saw him again. It was horrible to see him in such terror, but it must have been a lot worse to be Roberto. I couldn't imagine ever flying on a bomber with him.

As you might imagine, it got pretty dull around the apartment building once Roberto left, so late one night we sneaked into apartment #310 when everyone was asleep. We knew this wouldn't be a problem because no one had locks on their doors. We took their paper basket and put some newspapers in it, just enough for a small, quick fire that might scare the devil out of them. We lit the paper and left quickly. All of a sudden we could hear people yelling from the other side of the door, "Fire! Fire!" They all woke up in a panic and put out the fire. Some of the guys came running out of their rooms, wondering what the hell had happened, but we played totally dumb and didn't leave our apartment. As we were to find out, staying in our apartment when everyone else jumped outside was no doubt our biggest mistake.

The next day nothing much was said about the incident and we thought it was forgotten. But the following day when we got back from class, we found one of our dress shoes with a big turd in it. In fact, we soon discovered that each one of us had a polluted dress shoe. Our adversaries must have saved up all night and most of the day to produce turds that big. We knew we had been had. We cleaned out our shoes and didn't say a word about it. We didn't want to give them the satisfaction of knowing they had gotten to us. No one said a word to us, either. I guess they didn't want to antagonize us and escalate the conflict. You better believe we got rid of all our newspapers, pronto.

Somehow, all four of us fulfilled the requirements of the course and graduated. It was a wonder. I think we may have been the only roommates in the course who went through successfully together without a hitch. I guess we proved our intelligence in the turkey caper. Still, it was remarkable that we all passed. My God, Hanlin always had a pint of booze with him in the classroom. La Primo only seemed to worry about one thing: whether his girlfriend's mother was going to break up his relationship with her daughter. None of us were surprised that Hamilton passed. Heck, he had coordinated the turkey job and was the smartest out of the bunch. He graduated with a 97+ grade average. As for me, well I had never been a stellar student in school, but I really cared about passing this course. It was my ticket to getting action in the war and I wasn't going to miss it for the world. I graduated with an 85.76 average. Finally, the pressure of ending up in North Africa and washing sand off airplanes was over. I did hate to leave Miami and Coral Gables—they were both beautiful places. I hated to leave, but there was a war on.

Lowrey Field, Denver

At this point, I was separated from my three roommates. I was shipped to Lowrey Field, Denver, while they headed off to a new school in the Midwest. I guess they were more sane than I because they wanted no part of aerial gunner school. Before I was assigned to a crew, I traveled only by troop trains, so the travel time was pretty long. Everyone brought their kitchen supplies along because one car of the train had kitchen facilities. We slept in bunks on the train which were pretty uncomfortable but I still liked traveling on the rails. At least I got a good look at the country I was fighting for.

At Embry Riddle, my roommates and I had crammed for the theory work of aviation. Now in Denver and working at United Airlines, I was going to get onto the practical aspect of our training. We would actually get the chance to work on some of the airplanes, but only under the close supervision of their top mechanics.

It was ironic that I was working on airplanes but had never even flown in one. On one of my lunch breaks I was watching three guys who were climbing into a DC-3 (the Army Air Force called her a C-47). I asked them if I could go up because I had never flown before. They said, "Sure, we're going to practice landings and take-offs." I thought to myself, "Swell." I couldn't think of a better way to start than take-offs and landings. But what they didn't tell me was that they were also going to practice power stalls.

Power stalls! All I know about power stalls is the first time I experienced one, the airplane would start to climb without the pilot adding more power to the engines. A few moments later the plane would begin to shake and then it felt like it went into a swan dive. We were rushing toward the ground and I was convinced this was the end. I thought I would have to give up my life for my country in Denver, not the Pacific or European Theaters. No one else seemed scared though. Seemingly just before we hit the ground, the airplane pulled up again.

CHAPTER TWO

That's the only way I know how to describe a power stall. I got so sick to my stomach that I didn't care if we crashed or not. I just wanted to be off that airplane, one way or another. Only toward the end of the flight did they practice take-offs and landings. It wasn't a very promising beginning for someone who wanted to fly. I still believed to the core of my heart that as a tail gunner I could last longer than seventeen seconds in combat.

In Denver we worked with the United Airlines mechanics. They were well-schooled and very professional. We worked with them on the tail section, the fuselage, and the landing gears. We learned to remove and replace instruments. We would perform the twenty-five hours and fifty-hours inspection on the engines. The numbers stood for actual flying hours. We would check all cables, screws, nuts and bolts, and rivets. One time we changed an engine. I was amazed that only four bolts held that engine in place. For the most part, everything was routine in Denver. I never flew again until I arrived in Long Beach.

At United Airlines I met a lovely girl named Gina who worked in the main office. I thought she was very attractive. She wore glasses and in those days glasses weren't considered as attractive as they are today—there were only a few styles and the frames were sometimes so heavy that they covered your face too much. Gina was self-conscious of her glasses but I assured her she looked good in hers and I meant it. She had pretty features. Her eyes were widely spread and she had dark brown hair, full lips, a wide smile and always seemed to have a gleam in her eyes that the heaviest glasses couldn't possibly have obscured. She was about five-foot-three with a thin waist and what must have been a thirty-six-inch bust. She was twenty-one and seemed to be enjoying life for all it was worth.

Every time I got a chance, I would go over to talk to her to get an idea of what she was like, what she liked to do and whether she might want to join me on a date. One day she told me that she lived with her mother. She said she had a girlfriend and, if I could bring a friend, she would invite us over for an Italian dinner. I had no idea she was Italian. Lord knows, I was sick of pasta. During the Depression I had pasta with beans, pasta with cabbage, pasta with mushrooms and, sometimes, just plain pasta. My gosh, we must have eaten it five times a week. But why not? This girl seemed very nice and there was no doubt that she was very attractive, with a cute pug nose and beautiful brown hair. So I took the plunge, accepted and rounded up a friend to join me for pasta.

My buddy, Fred, and I got on a bus leaving from Lowrey Field. A little while later we were at the front door and ready, against my wishes, to eat pasta. When the door opened, there were our dates. Mine, cute as ever. His, Hazel, blond and just plain pretty. Heck, my buddy, who hadn't done a thing to earn this date, was in luck. Hazel, who lived a few blocks away, turned out to be good company and talked a lot with her hands. She was a little plump (probably from working in a bakery) and taller than Gina. After talking with the girls for a while, I felt completely at ease. Even Gina's teenage brother seemed like a nice, normal fellow who wasn't worried about protecting his sister's virtue.

Then we met the mother. I had met more than my fair share of Italian mothers in my day and she was just what I expected—short and buxom. In those days if an Italian woman was buxom it meant that she had had kids and that meant prestige. Unfortunately, it also meant that she aged fast and some of them lost their looks in their forties. This Italian mother was a widow, with a son in the Navy and another son still too young for the service.

Mama and I took over the conversation. She was telling me how worried she was about her son in the Navy. I told her she shouldn't worry because he was in the best Navy in the world. I did my best to reassure her, because her daughter was a doll and I needed someone like her while I was stationed in Denver. If she wasn't interested in fooling around, we could still have a terrific time. And if she was interested in fooling around, I figured she wasn't a risk for getting VD. I hadn't forgotten the films we had seen in Miami. We had a great time that night. I won the mother over, partly by eating a lot of food, an important compliment to pay to an Italian mother.

We did indeed have the usual pasta, but it was prepared somewhat differently from what I had grown up with. She used spareribs to make the tomato sauce. Those spareribs were delicious, and I ate more than my share. We also ate fried zucchini and had our salad last, in the Italian style. At dinner I didn't drink any wine because I still couldn't stand the smell.

After thanking Gina's mother for a great dinner, Fred and I took our dates on the bus to a dance that was being held at a nearby park. When we arrived, we discovered a large ballroom which could hold perhaps eight hundred people. When the music began they dimmed the lights, and the room was transformed with soft colors. There were a lot of single girls and some GIs like ourselves. These dances were a great way for guys and girls to meet. Sammy Kay's band was playing there that night. The band consisted of three trumpets, three trombones, four saxophones, a drum, a bass, a guitar and a piano. We spent a good couple of hours there dancing.

I liked dancing with Gina because it was obvious she liked to be held tight. By contrast, dancing with Hazel was like driving a truck. I had to steer her around the floor, and she just never seemed to shut up. Fred told me later that she drove him nuts, but for some reason he liked her. I told Fred there would be no more double dating between the four of us because I had a live one in Gina. After dancing, we caught the bus and brought the girls home. I set up another date with Gina on the way home. But for our next date, I picked a night I knew Fred had barracks duty!

A few days later I was knocking at Gina's door again. I expected to see her teenage brother all dressed up to tag along with us but he wasn't even home. Mama came to the door instead. I always felt a little uncomfortable around her because it seemed like she could read my mind before I had even thought of something. She had obviously spent too much time with Italian men. She would scrutinize me, as if to say, "I want my daughter back just the way you picked her up."

When Gina came out she looked great. She was wearing a blue and white blouse with a blue pleated skirt and a ribbon in her hair. I complimented Mama again on her dinner and told her how much I enjoyed the spareribs. She was all smiles and said, "Thatsa nice." She asked me if I wanted to use the family car for our date. My ears perked up. Having a car was something every GI dreams about having for a date. I have a feeling Mama wouldn't have offered me the car if she knew what was going to happen later.

We finally left in the 1937 four-door Chevrolet. During the war, gasoline was rationed and everyone was given a stamp that allowed them to purchase four gallons a week for pleasure driving. That was okay by me, because the place we were headed was only about a mile and a half away.

When we had driven about a block away from the house, Gina pulled a pack of cigarettes out of her purse and lit up. She hadn't done this on our first date, maybe because she didn't want Hazel to know that she smoked. She moved over and sat very close to me. This I liked. I thought about her mother. If she could only see us now! What Mama didn't know wouldn't hurt her. We went to a place called Elitches. I surveyed the area, wondering if there was any place around us where we could park after the dance. I didn't know that Gina had already made plans for us.

Elitches was a beautiful place. The ballroom was the most exquisite I had ever seen. The colors were all bright blue, silver and red. The lighting was something I'd never seen before. During intermission, the place was all lit up, but when you were dancing they would dim the lights and constantly change the colors, which transformed the place into a kind of wonderland. There were sofas and chairs to sit, with chairs set up around the edge of the dance floor, similar to the previous place we had been. No matter where we were, we could get a good view of the band, because the dance floor was low, and everything else was elevated over it. Joe Reichman and his band were playing there. Gina and I jitter-bugged, got in a conga line, danced cheek to cheek, even danced to a waltz. During one of the intermissions we went out to the car and I got a little excited. She told me to wait until later. I had no idea she had planned every-thing out.

A little while later we left the dance. In the car she moved over and said to me, "Take me home." I said, "Home!" She looked at me archly and replied, "You'll see." She kept looking at me, half laughing and half smiling.

Her mother's house was old, with a garage under-neath it, next to the basement. From the garage, a door led to the basement. When we arrived the garage doors were still open. There weren't even locks on garage doors in those days! She told me to drive into the garage. Talk about disappointed. I sighed, drove in and turned off the lights. Then she said, "We can do it here."

I yelled out, "What?"

"Shhhh," she said. "My mother's sleeping."

I just looked at her and said, "Hell, no, we can't do it here. Are you crazy?"

She said, "My mother is a sound sleeper. She very seldom comes down to the basement, let alone the garage."

I did not like the word "seldom" one bit. It only took once, I knew, and we would be in a helluva lot of trouble. But Gina was so calm, so sure of herself, she eventually calmed me down. I was still plenty nervous. I told her I could not possibly perform. I could just see her mama opening the door, turning on the light and saying, "Is that you, Eddie?"

Calmly, and in a low voice, Gina said, "You have nothing to worry about. We have no bullets for the gun." I said, "Thanks for sharing that." I was fit to be tied. She kept on playing around with me, and this was hard to resist.

Finally, she got out of the car and took off her blouse and bra. Then she put her blouse back on but didn't button it. She then got in the back seat. I figured, what the hell, sooner or later everyone dies. Besides, I didn't want to live forever.

Although I was in a state of shock, my thing was still like a rocket ready to be launched. I got into the back seat and on top of Gina. While we were doing it, I kept looking up at the basement door. Under those circumstances, it was a quickie. I pulled up my shorts and pants, buckled up and said, "If you want to talk to me, I'll be halfway up the block."

I got the hell out of that garage as quickly as I could. I was more scared in that garage than I ever would be in a cloud of flak over Germany. A minute later she met me up the block. I told her, "Don't you ever, ever ask me to do that again. Never! Never!" She just laughed. I don't believe this girl feared anything. I told her we would have to make other plans for the future. She said she would think of something.

On my arrival back at the base, I told some of the guys what had happened. The ones who believed me couldn't stop laughing. Fred himself could hardly believe me. He just said, "That takes guts."

When I arrived for my third date with Gina, I walked into the house and the mother gave me a funny look. Right away I said to myself, "Oh no, her daughter couldn't have told her about what we did." Then I thought it was a good thing her daddy wasn't alive—he might get pretty belligerent. I had heard in those days that in some places in Italy if you got into a daughter's pants and didn't follow it up with marriage, the father might shoot you and not worry about the authorities stepping in for punishment. I don't know if this is true or not, but if we had been in Italy I would have thought twice about making love to a girl I didn't plan to marry.

Mama took me into her daughter's bedroom and led me to her hope chest. Hope chests were a kind of dowry—girls put together all their personal essentials for when they got married. Here were the usual things: sheets, pillow cases, table cloths, blankets, nighties and panties. But I had already seen those! Mama said to me in broken English, "Hey you, you come here for business or monkey business?" I was a little bit shocked, but I suppose it was a fair question. She only had her daughter's best interest in mind.

I told her, "Your daughter is very beautiful and a sweet girl who will eventually make her husband very happy. He'll be a lucky man—but I'm not in the husband sweepstakes. I'm in the service and will be shipped out of Denver soon."

"In that case," she said, "you can take my daughter to the dance, but no *monkey business*." And boy, she meant it. I had three condoms in my pocket and I would have given almost anything to throw two of them in the hope chest, but I didn't get the chance. I figured Mama would have a helluva time explaining two condoms to the next guy for whom she opened up the hope chest.

Gina and I dated a few more times. She borrowed the keys of a girlfriend's apartment who worked nights in an ammunition factory. About ten days after our third date, Uncle Sam intervened in the monkey business. I had completed my training course and was about to be shipped off to Long Beach. I was happy to leave Denver. I told Gina I was going overseas soon, but that if I was ever in Denver again I would visit her—but you had better believe I never visited her garage again.

Long Beach, California

When I arrived in Long Beach, the first thing I did was to inquire about Aerial Gunner School. I was still determined to be a tail gunner, seventeen seconds or not. I wanted to know how I would react to flying combat missions—hopefully better than I had the first time I went up in the air, which made me sick as a dog. For some silly reason, I wanted to know what it was like to be shot at in an airplane, thousands of feet in the air. Could I take it or not?

Long Beach had an enormous air base. On one side was the Douglas Aircraft Company, churning out planes for the war effort twenty-four hours a day. I was assigned to a C-47 army version of the Douglas DC-3, a twin-engine cargo or passenger plane. I was the engineer. We also had an instructor pilot and radio operator. We were supposed to check out pilots on the C-47. My job was to inspect the plane before starting and taking off.

The instructor pilot always sat in the co-pilot's seat. Any pilot we were checking out would sit in the pilot's seat. Usually, I would stand between the pilots checking instruments and, on landings, call off air speeds. On take off, when we would start to climb, the instructor pilot would pull back the gas throttle on one of the engines. The student pilot had to react quickly to push up the throttle on the live engine to give us more power and to feather the prop of the supposedly dead engine. Up in the air, we would fly over Signal Hill, which was covered with oil derricks. We could see them immediately after take off. More than once, we'd fly alongside a derrick, not over it. It could get a little scary. Flying alongside an oil derrick with both engines running was no problem. But when we flew next to one with only one engine, we might have been only eight hundred feet off the ground.

In order for a pilot to be able to fly the C-47, he had to be checked out on many things, like flying on one engine, taking off and landing, instrument flying, plus getting the feel for an aircraft. The instructor pilots really grilled the student pilots to see if they could handle the pressure and possessed the incredible technical knowledge required at that time.

Also stationed at Long Beach were WASPs— Women Airforce Service Pilots. Because the military draft didn't apply to women, WASPs were volunteers. They were true patriots. I believe WASPs represented the first time in aviation history that women flew airplanes during wartime.

WASP missions began in 1942, when the Air Transport Command began under the government's flying plan. I know one thing, they didn't get any special treatment. In the Army, there's one way to do just about everything, and these women were taught the Army way, I'm sure.

Over eleven hundred WASPs graduated from flight training school. They were taught how to fly cargo planes, fighter planes, two-engine and four-engine bombers. They even trained how to fly the B-29, the super fortress, which was the biggest plane around at the time. I met a woman at Long Beach who had ferried a P-39 to Fairbanks, Alaska. There the Russian women pilots would pick them up and fly to Russia. My friend had also flown planes which towed targets that were being fired on thirty yards to her rear. Once I became a tail gunner and flew combat missions, I wondered if she had ever returned from her target duties with holes in the plane. WASPs logged over sixty million air miles during the war. Like just about everyone else, I admired the WASPs very much. And the one WASP I got to know well was smart, tough, young and beautiful. That's a formidable combination.

One day I was in the gym working out, when one of the women pilots asked me if I would like to be her partner in a badminton mixed couple league. Only a fool would have said no. She was a pretty blonde with dimples. Her name was Shelly. It didn't look like there was an ounce of fat on her. She was twenty-two. I don't know why I was the lucky stiff she asked, but I was sure glad she did. She was from Tucson, Arizona, and she had aspirations of becoming a commercial pilot after the war was over. She knew, though, that there would be a glut of pilots then.

We played badminton together a lot and did well. I wanted to do more than just play badminton, though, but her duties always seemed to get in the way. Consequently, we didn't see a lot of each other. Whenever I got the chance I would take her to a club near the field, called the "Bomber Shelter," for drinks and dinner. One

CHAPTER TWO

memorable night I met her at the PX (Post Exchange), and asked her if she would like to go to a movie the following night. She said yes. I was a very happy man because I knew she didn't have an Italian mama (or papa) looking over my shoulder.

The following night I picked her up, and we grabbed a bite to eat at the PX, planning to head out for a movie afterwards. All of a sudden, a blackout was called. There were rumors that a Japanese sub had been spotted along the Southern California coast. Luckily for me, my badminton partner's roommate was ferrying a plane back east, so she was alone for the night. I bought some beer, and we went to her quarters. We lit a candle and turned on the radio to listen to some beautiful music. I had expected to be sitting next to her all night in the movie theater, but somehow I was alone with a beautiful woman in her quarters. To hell with the movie, to hell with the Japanese sub, to hell with the VD film. We just "banged" the night away. After that, we depended a lot on her roommate being away on a flight in order to be alone.

In those days, romances were always brief. You never got too serious with anyone because there was never time. You never knew when you might be shipped out and never see each other again. You couldn't afford to get emotionally involved with anyone because, while they might be here today, they were gone—either transferred or dead—tomorrow. Sometimes we would be stationed at a base and a fellow might meet a girl, fall in love and then marry just before they were shipped out. I would never have done that. Still, Shelly is one girl that I would have loved to have seen after the war. But like most people who met in those crazy times, we didn't plan anything.

Shortly after the escapade with my badminton partner, I was told I would be shipped to Harlingen, Texas to attend aerial gunner school. I was so excited. I still had some time before beginning training, though, so in order to keep me busy while waiting for reassignment, I was told to drive a jeep from morning until noon. At Long Beach, the field had military planes on one side and civilian planes on the other. The jeep I drove had a sign on the back of it that said, "Follow me." If a military plane landed, I would drive onto the runway and, with my sign in place, direct the plane to its parking spot. Eventually, I did the same with the civilian planes.

At the time, a Hollywood studio was on the base filming *Ladies Courage*, a story about women fliers, starring Loretta Young. I was asked to drive the jeep past the camera so they could read the "Follow me" sign. They were pretending that a military plane was landing and wanted a realistic shot for the film. This was my big chance! Maybe I was going to be discovered. Maybe I was going to be a star. I drove in front of the camera twice. How could I not end up in the picture?

Besides Loretta Young, there was an actress on site by the name of Ann Gwyne. She was beautiful, with deep dimples. At this time, the Air Force had its own airlines called SNAFU. One of these planes was parked nearby, and I was hanging around the film crew hoping to be discovered, when Ann approached me and asked what SNAFU meant. I told her, "Situation Normal All Fouled Up," except that they were already using the other four letter F-word back then. I didn't think I should bring it up to Ann, though. I sure wanted to take her home, but I'm afraid she wasn't interested.

A few years after the war, I saw *Ladies Courage* on TV. The first couple of minutes of the film you could see the damn jeep with its sign, but you couldn't see me. No wonder I never got a phone call.

Harlingen, Texas

After waiting around in Long Beach for what seemed like an eternity, I was finally shipped to Harlingen, Texas to attend aerial gunner school. This was why I had entered the war. This was my combat destiny. Harlingen had a beautiful field. In the autumn of 1943, the place wasn't too hot. It had a nice breeze from the Gulf.

Just after the new group of trainees arrived in Texas, we were briefed on what our schooling would look like. Training would not only include the usual written tests but more unusual things: We would have to take a .50-caliber machine gun apart and put it back together blindfolded—we had to know that gun inside out. We had to learn how to identify friendly and enemy aircraft after seeing them for 1/25th of a second on screen. The instructors had to be nuts! Somehow though, I learned to take the machine gun apart and put it back again. In time, I could also identify friendly and enemy aircraft in the minimal time allotted. On the final test, I got ninety-six out of one hundred correct. Twice I mistook the Zeke for the Zero, and the Zero for the Zeke. The only important thing was that they were both enemy aircraft, and if I saw them, I would do my best to blow them out of the sky.

We trained in the AT-13 (Advanced Trainer) single-engine airplane. There were only two of us in the plane —the pilot in the front seat and me in the back with a .30-caliber machine gun. We would fly low over the Gulf of Mexico and practice strafing. Then we would practice shooting targets towed by another aircraft. Slowly, I was learning how to aim ahead of our target to gain better accuracy.

One day in class the instructor asked the fellow next to me what he would do if he had a runaway machine gun. A runaway gun is one which, after you take your finger off the trigger, keeps firing. The answer was simple. All you have to do is lift the top latch and it will stop firing. My neighbor answered differently, though. He said, "I'd chase it, sir." The response was so unexpected that I started to laugh and couldn't stop. Finally, the instructor told me to get out in the hall and compose myself. Needless to say, the clever fellow next to me didn't make it. They kicked him out. I always wondered if he ended up washing sand off planes in North Africa.

One of the tests we were given didn't feel like a test at all to me. I was placed in a small black room with no windows. I noticed a bench with a pad on it. When they shut and locked the door, I noticed it was so black in the room that I couldn't even see my hand. I managed to make it over to the bench, lie down on the pad and fall asleep.

After a while someone opened the door and took a look at me. The light from outside woke me up. He shut the door again and locked it. I fell back to sleep. A while later they came in and woke me up. They said, "Come on, it's time for lunch." I must have been in there all morning, for about three hours. For the life of me, I couldn't figure out why they had done this. They didn't tell me a thing. But I knew at least I was well-rested for the remainder of the day. A couple of days later I saw one of the guys that had put me in the room. I asked what they were looking for. "We wanted to see if you would panic," he said. "If you panic, we want you down here, not up there," pointing up at the sky. Suddenly, everything made sense to me.

I guess they performed this test on me because the tail turret was a truly compact piece of machinery. It was an armor structure with an armor plate glass in front of my face for protection. The whole turret revolved from within and included two mounted .50-caliber machine guns. Some machine gun turrets could be either hydraulically or manually operated. I happened to be in an Emerson-made turret. It was hydraulically operated and three different times our hydraulic system was shot out. Fortunately, the manual system acted as a backup.

In those days I was about five-foot-eight and weighed 165 pounds. I wore a heated flying suit so my butt wouldn't freeze off and a "Mae West" a flotation vest in case we hit the water. My flying gear also included a parachute harness and a heavy flak jacket. Today if I tried to get into that turret with all of that equipment, I would be lucky if I could get my legs in. Tail gunners couldn't wear their parachute because of the lack of space. They kept their chutes directly in back of the turret. If I ever had to get out of the bomber in a hurry I would throw myself backwards out of the turret, take off my flak jacket, and hook the chute onto the harness. Timing myself once, I determined I could do all of this in six seconds.

Sitting in the tail turret made it impossible to see any other part of the aircraft. It was like hanging over a cliff—you could only see where you had been, not where you were going. When you were on your bomb run with the bomb bay doors open, you had to stay steady on course no matter what. Sometimes the nose gunner would call out, "Flak at ten o'clock low!" or "one o'clock high." That wasn't so bad. But when you heard, "Flak at twelve o'clock level!" you got sick to your stomach. You knew you had to fly right through it.

Once when flying in a tight formation on our way to bomb an ammunition plant at Hamm, Germany, an enemy ME 109 fighter screeched through our formation firing a shell and hitting the wing gas tank of the bomber flying on my left. The bomber exploded. Debris of that aircraft tore off half of our right rudder, ripping two holes in the fuselage just inches behind my turret. Somehow, I never got a scratch. What's it like flying in the tail of a B-24 Liberator? I would say that if you're able to get back home to talk about it, it was a piece of cake. For too many tail gunners in World War II, it wasn't a piece of cake at all.

I wasn't too worried about heights. Heck, one time after drinking with a bunch of my buddies, I bet one of them that I could climb the base water tower faster than he could. He took me up on it. Before we could get to the top, the MPs were on the scene. They ordered us down, but we refused, so they had to come up and get us. I guess I was better on take-offs than landings.

The MPs didn't throw us in the brig or anything like that. They came up with a much more creative punishment. Abbott and Costello were a popular comic team heard over the radio and seen in the movies during the war. Of course Abbott was the straight man and he was always giving Costello hell for screwing things up. Costello would always say the same thing, "I'm a bad boy." So my buddy and I got the Abbott and Costello treatment.

Let me explain what I mean. At the end of the base there were four barracks. These were the Women Air Corps (WAC) quarters. WACs were stationed there in order to perform most of the base's office duties. With the WACs firmly in mind, the MPs sentenced us to something worse than a public flogging. We had to spend the whole day (with time out only for lunch) marching up and down in front of the WAC barracks with a big, heavy sign that said, "I am a bad boy." We were the butt of WAC jokes all day long. Boy, did I feel stupid! That was the last time I ever tried to climb a water tower.

Salt Lake City, Utah

Despite the water tower incident, I somehow graduated from aerial gunner school and was shipped out to Salt Lake City in order to be assigned to a crew.

I met the B-24 crew that I would spend more or less the rest of the war with. I immediately knew that I was fortunate to be teamed up with a bunch of guys I both liked and respected. Our crew would fly numerous successful missions together (though I only put in thirty-three, but that's another story). I could see that we all shared a good sense of humor, which I figured was important in a war. Maybe the only exception to this was the pilot, who had a serious side to him. This would turn out to be the best thing in the world for us because he made it clear from the start that we had to do a first-rate job in order some day to tell war stories like this one.

I wanted to be assigned to a heavy bomber, provided it was a B-17. I caught wind of the fact that we weren't going to be assigned to a B-17 at all, but a B-24 Liberator. I had a fit. Livid, I was granted permission to speak to a captain. I told him I was from Seattle, where they built the B-17, and I wanted badly to be assigned to one. He looked at me funny, as if to say, "Where in the hell did we pick this guy up?" He told me, "You're assigned to a B-24 and you'll stay on a B-24 as long as you don't get blown out of the sky."

I really told him off. I said, "Yes, sir."

They couldn't order us to fly combat missions against our will. It was strictly voluntary. But I wouldn't have quit for anything, so I was stuck on a B-24 and we were shipped out to Nebraska for crew training.

The B-24 Liberator was a four-engine, long-range bomber. The B-24s our group flew had Pratt & Whitney engines. The Consolidated Aircraft Company of San Diego first started building these B-24s. In 1942, Corvair of Fort Worth, Texas, took over the B-24 contract. Later on, Douglas did the same thing, building the planes in Tulsa, Oklahoma, of all places. Finally, the B-24 ended up being built at Willow Run by Ford. The B-24 we were assigned to was built at Willow Run. We understood that Ford was putting out one B-24 bomber every sixty-three minutes. With that kind of output and no fear of bombing from abroad, there was just no way the German war machine could keep up with us.

Because it was so large, the B-24 was sometimes used as a cargo carrier. In front was the nose turret with its two .50-caliber machine guns. In back of the nose turret and in front of the cockpit was the bombardier with his bomb sight and the navigator with his navigational equipment. In the cockpit above the nose were the pilot on the left and the copilot on the right, with their instrument panel and switches. Between the pilots were the four engine throttles. Two .50-caliber machine guns were located in the top turret directly behind the cockpit. Underneath the top turret were fuse boxes and switches to transfer gas from one tank to another as needed.

Behind the top turret and down the right side of the aircraft sat the radio operator. His radio rested on a small table, and on his left was a small window he could look out of. After this came the bomb bay, where the bombs were housed. On the bomb runs, the radio man would travel down from his station and open the bomb bay doors with a lever. He would wait for the bombs to be released by the bombardier, then he would close the doors. Where he knelt waiting for the bombs to drop was a small pipe through which all the plane's hydraulic fluid flows and disperses itself to the various hydraulic units on board.

In back of the bomb bay doors was the belly turret with its two .50-caliber machine guns. On each side of this were the two waist gunners, each with his own .50-caliber machine gun. Then there was me in the tail. Between the waist gunner and me, there was an escape hatch, a flat door which we could open to get in or out of the plane, or to bail out if the plane was going down. On board were four oxygen tanks, with twenty minutes of oxygen each. There was one in the nose, one in the cockpit and two with us in the back. We also had something called a "Gravel Gertie," which could send out a very strong radio beam if the plane went down over either land or sea.

CHAPTER TWO

Edgar Spencer, Pilot

In introducing the crew, I should start with the pilot, Edgar Spencer. He's first because, honestly, more than anyone else, he was the reason I'm able to write this memoir today. Edgar was a mature twenty-seven, the oldest of the crew. He stood about six feet tall, was of medium weight and had a lot of hair. He expected absolute perfection out of the crew, and he damn near got it. He was such a perfectionist that he not only knew his own tasks like the back of his hand, he knew everyone else's, too. Maybe Edgar's only recognizable fault was that he was a heavy smoker. Every member of the crew received a whopping seven packs of cigarettes a week. I didn't smoke and, wanting to keep Edgar happy, I gave him my packs. Edgar was no freeloader, and he offered candy bars or money in exchange for the cigarettes. But I figured it was smart to keep Edgar on my side if at all possible, so I simply told him, "You can have them." Cigarettes in those days were worth about twenty cents a pack, but it was more than worth the sacrifice in money to get in good with my pilot, who wanted to have the best American flight crew in England, no small feat with all of the competition.

In the plane, Edgar sat at twelve o'clock. As the tail gunner, I sat at six o'clock. After takeoff we used to join the formation. The leader would always shoot red flares, so if we knew where the leader was, we knew where our position was, and we could form accordingly. One day—I'm almost ashamed to admit it—we were getting into position over England, and I was actually reading an Archie comic book. It was my attitude that we weren't going to be shot at in Allied territory so why sweat it? Edgar called me over the intercom and inquired, "Do you see any red flares?"

I replied, "Nope."

Then he said in a controlled voice, "Try looking at seven o'clock high," so I did and, sure enough, there were the red flares, just like Edgar said. He followed up his advantage. "I know you're reading a comic book. Get rid of that damn thing, now!" Edgar was so sharp that at the twelve o'clock position he could actually spot the flares that I hadn't spotted. He could even spot my comic book.

On take-offs I was always in the back of the plane, so I never saw much of what went on in the cockpit. How formally religious Edgar was I don't know, but I do know that he wore a St. Christopher medal bracelet around his wrist. The boys up front said that just before every take off Edgar would straighten out the medal so that he could see it facing him. I don't know how much stock to put in St. Christopher, but I'm sure glad that Edgar did what he did.

Another story illustrates Edgar's complete professionalism. One day coming out of France, we had lost an engine and another one was sputtering along at half power. From the tail I spotted some B-17s coming home, so we flew under them to get their fighter support. In order to do that we had to give them the code of the day, because sometimes the Germans would repair old Allied planes and bring them up as a primitive kind of "stealth" fighter. Nearly desperate, we threw everything possible out of the airplane to make it lighter, except the ammunition and the parachutes.

By the time we reached the English Channel the B-17s had left us, and we were left alone. During that era when Allied planes flew over the greater London area alone—an enormous area even then—we had to give the air defense teams on the ground the code of the day, which entailed flashing a series of lights from the airplane. If we didn't give them an accurate code, they would simply shoot a plane down, no questions asked. I had just extricated myself from the tail turret after about seven consecutive hours there, when all of a sudden a barrage of flak fired around us. What the devil? We were over England, not Germany for Christ's sake! Calmly as usual, Edgar hailed our radio operator, who was responsible for the code. "Did you give them the code of the day?" and the radio operator replied, sheepishly, "I don't know it." Luckily for all of us the pilot—the pilot!—actually had taken the trouble to learn the code, and he delivered it in a hurry from the cockpit. If he hadn't known the code, the war would have been cut short for all of us. Let me tell you, Edgar Spencer was very sharp.

Frank Collela, Copilot

The copilot was a guy named Frank Collela. Like me he was single and Italian. Unlike me, he was from New York City, like most Italians in the American popular imagination. Collela was of medium height and build, and boy, did he look the part of the Italian from New York. He was a very talented flyer. On bombing missions he would fly the plane manually in formation. Without question he was one of the most accomplished formation pilots in the group. He was also very superstitious —so often, the most proficient people are the ones who are superstitious. He never, ever liked to discuss the future, and he always had to be the last one out of bed in the morning. At least that's what I was told. We enlisted men had our own huts and officers had their own quarters. When the officers from our crew used to come around we would tell them kiddingly, "Beat it! This place is for enlisted men, not officers." It was the only time we ever really had any authority over them.

Peter Moskovitis, Top Turret Gunner

Peter Moskovitis, the top turret gunner, was everybody's favorite crew member. He hailed from Milwaukee, Wisconsin. When we were stationed in Casper, Wyoming, his girlfriend from Milwaukee met him there and they got married, either a brave or stupid thing to do before going off to war. When we first started flying bombing missions, Pete was extremely nervous and had a tendency to talk very loud and fast over the intercom. I used to implore him to talk slower and softer. As we flew more missions, though, he became better and better until he got almost downright cocky. Every time we would return from a bombing mission, Pete would paint a bomb

CHAPTER TWO

onto his leather bomber jacket. When we returned from our thirty-first mission we were informed that we probably had two more left in us, because replacement flyers were coming in. Pete figured, "What the heck?" and painted two more bombs on his jacket. Superstitious Frank caught wind of the fact that there were bombs on Pete's jacket for missions we hadn't flown yet. He was livid and made Pete get rid of those bombs. Pete, who truly did have a heart of gold, felt bad and took a razor blade and scraped off those two bombs. Frank wouldn't leave until he saw Pete scrape them off. Superstitions aside, Frank Colella was a great pilot.

Pete was a charming piece of work. On each mission we were issued escape kits with French money and pictures of us in street clothes, so that if we were shot down, the French Underground could give us an identity. They also gave us K-rations. This included cigarettes, chocolate, a can of corned beef or hash or Spam. Sometimes, if we were lucky, we would get a can of cheese and bacon bits which was everybody's favorite K-ration meal.

On one particular mission we were supposed to fly in between two cities because it was the shortest route into the target. If we were accurately on course, the flak could not touch us. As it turned out, Colella and Spencer piloted the bomber straight and true. We dropped our bombs and headed home. That day I happened to receive the K-ration with the cheese and bacon bits, the only one among the crew to have it. During the flight back to England, the intercom was quieter than usual because everyone was anxious about flying between the two cities and whether or not we would be shot at. Suddenly, out of the quiet came Pete's voice over the intercom, "Hey Picardo, would you trade me my corned beef for your cheese and bacon?" When we landed Spencer was hysterical with laughter. He said, "Here is the guy we were worried about the most, and now he's the calmest one of the bunch." Pete was such a terrific guy and his request for a trade was so funny that there was no way I could turn him down. He ate bacon bits and cheese that day.

One morning on the base, I was about to take a shower, but I noticed I was out of shampoo. On Pete's shelf behind his bunk was a large bottle of Fitch shampoo, so I borrowed it. When I started to shampoo my hair, though, I couldn't get any suds. Then I realized it wasn't what I thought it was. It was booze! His wife had shipped it to him from the States. I never said a word and slipped it back on the shelf without anyone seeing me.

Winter in England was cold and foggy, and our hut had just a small woodstove to keep us warm. I figured that if no one was around, I could help myself to a couple of shots to keep myself warm, which I did now and then.

One morning we were sleeping in, and part of our group was on a bombing mission. One of our bombers tried to return to the base, having lost both engines on their left wing. When the pilot came in for a landing, he banked his aircraft on the left where the dead engines were. The aircraft went straight down, hitting the ground near our hut. There was one hell of an explosion. It woke us up and scared the hell out of all of us. It blew open the

Left:
Ernesto, Grandma
and Grandpa. 1899

Below:
The Picardo Clan at Picardo
Farm—Eddie in little car in the
lower left corner. 1928

Right:
The Picardo clan
with my mother
as a little girl on
the far right.

Above:
Georgia Picardo
and Dean Guintoli's
wedding pictures.
May 20th, 1939

Left:
Eddie's family
L to R: Bob, Mother
Georgina, Eddie, Norma,
Father Edward and
Lorraine. Eddie's mother
is pregnant with Jackie.

Right:
Grandma's
stucco house.
Eddie on tricycle
beside Grandpa.

Right:
L to R—back: Eddie's Mother, Georgia Picardo Sauro, Grandma and Mary Picardo.
Front: Darling little boy, Eddie Picardo, Georgina Picardo Guintoli and my brother, Bob Picardo.

Above:
Sicks' Seattle Stadium. Home of the Seattle Rainiers: Seattle's Pacific Coast league baseball team.

Left:
Uncle Fred, Grandpa and Uncle Al.

While in pursuit of an airplane mechanics course, this group is seen undergoing its weekly personnel inspection by Lt. Donald H. Williams, one of the inspection officers of the AAFTTC Detachment at the Embry-Riddle School of Aviation. (Photo by Arthur Ruhnke)

Above Left:
Photo from article on Embry Riddle School of Aviation.

Above Right:
Embry Riddle School of Aviation. Miami, Florida.

TECHNICAL TRAINING COMMAND SCHOOL
CIVILIAN MECHANICS BRANCH

EMBRY-RIDDLE SCHOOL OF AVIATION

.........MIAMI, FLORIDA.........

CERTIFICATE OF
TECHNICAL TRAINING

Date. March 26, 1943....

This is to certify that:

PICARDO........EDDIE........S.
(Surname)   (Christian)   (Middle)

20945603   PFC   A.C.
(Serial No.) (Rank)   (Org. or Arm)

Graduated from the

AIRCRAFT INSPECTION & MAINTENANCE COURSE

on....March 26, 1943......

with rating of

....Very Satisfactory.....

Subjects covered and grades on same
are shown on reverse side.

By order of:

....OLIVER H. McKEOWN.....
GAPT. AIR CORPS.

Director of Training.

(Furnished in compliance with paragraph 2 a (6) (c) AR 350-5)

A.B.C. Form 18

Left and Right:
Front and back of Eddie's School of Aviation report card. 1943

SUBJECTS COVERED	HOURS	FINAL GRADE
BASIC INSTRUCTION	56	84.5
ELECTRICAL SYSTEMS	56	82
INSTRUMENTS	56	73.5
INDUCTION, FUEL & OIL	56	80.5
RADIAL ENGINES	56	83.5
PRIMAR STRUCTURES	56	92
HYDRAULICS	56	92.5
PROPELLERS	56	87.8
ENGINE TEST	56	83.5
DAILY PREFLIGHT	56	94
25-HR. INSPECTION	56	91.8
50-HR. INSPECTION	61	87.5

Total Hours............. 677

Final Weighted Grade............. 85.78

REMARKS:

Good student. Recommend Engine
Line Mechanics.

Right:
Diploma received
on completion of
aircraft inspection
and maintenance
course at Embry
Riddle School
of Aviation.

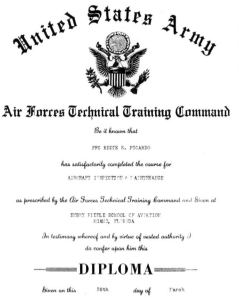

United States Army

Air Forces Technical Training Command

Be it known that

PFC EDDIE S. PICARDO

has satisfactorily completed the course for

AIRCRAFT INSPECTION AND MAINTENANCE

as prescribed by the Air Forces Technical Training Command and Given at

EMBRY RIDDLE SCHOOL OF AVIATION
MIAMI, FLORIDA

In testimony whereof and by virtue of vested authority I
do confer upon him this

═══ DIPLOMA ═══

Given on this   26th   day of   March

in the year of our Lord one thousand nine hundred and forty three

Captain, Air Corps
COMMANDING OFFICER
ARMY AIR FORCES TRAINING DETACHMENT

Left:
Uncle Al and Eddie, home on
leave before gunnery school.
1942

Above:
Eddie and the boys clowning for
the camera.

Above:
L to R: Top row: John Beavers, Navigator; Frank Collela, Co Pilot; Edgar
Spencer, Pilot; Bill Crean; Bombardier. Bottom row: Henry Fishbone, Radio
Operator; Eddie; Tom Stewart, Waist Gunner; Bob Burdick, Belly Gunner;
Pete Moskovitis, Top Turret Gunner; George Schofield, Waist Gunner.

Left:
Eddie receiving his Air Medal with
four oak leaf clusters. 1944

Below:
Eddie's Certificate of Valor. Awarded
for completion of his tour of duty in
World War II.

CERTIFICATE OF VALOR

It is an honor to give this testimonial of the performance of duty of
Staff Sergeant Eddie S. Picardo
who has completed an operational tour in the European Theater of
Operations with this Group and acquitted himself with valor.
He made a notable contribution to the success of the Armed Forces
of our Country.

December 21, 1944

Eugene H. Snavely

AWARDS
*Air Medal with
Four Oak Leaf Clusters*

Colonel - Air Corps
Commanding
44th Bombardment Group.

Above:
Eddie—If shot down the French Underground would use this for identification.

Left:
Horseback riding on leave.

Right:
Pete and Eddie on the balcony of their room at the castle. 1944

Above:
Eddie on R and R. 1944

Above:
Georgie Guintoli and
Louise Kennedy.

Above:
Eddie and his Mother at her
grandchild's wedding. 1979

Left:
Donna's University of Washington
Graduation.

Above:
Sarah, Grandpa and Jessica at home. 1994

back door of our hut, knocking the chimney off our stove and hurling equipment from our shelves. Smoke and soot were everywhere.

We all ran outside, wondering what had happened. It was a relief to see that our crew was all right. Then I saw it. The Fitch shampoo bottle on the ground was still intact. I gently picked it up and replaced it on Pete's shelf. Those were the good parts. The sad part was that nine telegrams would be sent out: "Killed in Action."

John Beavers, Navigator

The navigator, John Beavers, was a terrific guy too, though for whatever reason I don't remember him as well as some of the other fellas. He was a tall, slim, blonde kid from one of the Carolinas. His job, obviously, was to make sure we stayed on course. He was very good at his job, always careful to let us know exactly where we were at all times. He used to come visit us a lot with the bombardier in our hut.

Once while starting our bomb run, John leaned over to pick up something off the floor. While doing so his flack jacket unhooked falling to the floor. He stepped over to pick it up just as a shell penetrated from the bottom of our nose section right where John had been standing, ripping out our nose oxygen system. The shell forced itself through the top of our nose section about three feet in front of the cockpit and finally exploded. Pete our Engineer and top turret gunner rushed oxygen bottles to our crew members in the nose.

Just seconds before we dropped our bombs John looked from what we call a "blister," a bubble you could put your head in for better observation, when he saw a 500 pound bomb being dropped on top of another B-24. It exploded destroying the bomber and the crew.

He had many sleepless nights because of this. I admired our navigator John Beavers very much. They don't come any better.

Bill Crean, Bombardier

The bombardier was a smiling wonder named Bill Crean. Like John, he was tall, but heavy-set and single. He hailed from Pitkin Avenue in Someplace, New York. The reason I remember his street and not his city is because I heard a million times how after the war he was going to walk up and down Pitkin Avenue in his uniform. Twice at high altitude his oxygen mask became unhooked from the tube supplying oxygen, and he passed out. Once we had to give him mouth-to-mouth resuscitation. This was serious, but I never understood how he could act so unconcerned about it all. After the second time it happened, members of the crew took turns calling him to check to see that he was okay.

Bob Burdick, Belly Gunner

Our belly turret gunner, Bob, was single and was from the Midwest. When we arrived in England, though, they removed the belly turrets of the B-24s. This helped make the B-24 faster. The B-24 already had a longer range and carried a larger bomb load than the B-17s. So Bob was placed on guard duty and never even got to fly a mission with us, despite all of the training he had gone through. We didn't see a lot of him after that, but we did stay in touch occasionally.

Tom Stewart, Waist Gunner

Tom Stewart was our waist gunner. He was single and from Rochester, New York. I appreciated his guts and his positive attitude. The only time I ever heard him complain about anything was when they made him a tail gunner. If he were anywhere else in the plane, he was thrilled to be flying and always joked around. Tom was great, but he absolutely refused to fly the tail.

George Scofield, Waist Gunner

George Scofield was the other waist gunner. He was married and lived in Elizabeth City, New Jersey. Once on a bombing mission over Germany, we were in the bucket (or the slot, as some people called it). We had two wing men, one on our left and one on our right. The wing man on the left could not keep his plane in there steady, and he kept flying over us. Sometimes he was so close we could read the lettering on his plane, and that lettering was only one and a half inches tall. Scofield, who was a nervous wreck, called Edgar on the intercom and told him to tell that pilot to keep his plane away from us or else. Edgar did just that, but it didn't seem to make any difference.

Scofield said to me, "Why don't you give him a few bursts, Picardo?" In other words, he wanted me to shoot above them. Every third bullet was a tracer and you could see it, but I told him that only the waist gunner and the top turret gunner would be able to see my tracers. I said, "If you fire from the waist, the pilot of that plane will see the tracers from the cockpit." Edgar heard what we were saying and didn't say a word of warning to us. So Scofield did as I suggested, firing several rounds directly above the cockpit.

Their pilot called Edgar over the radio to ask him what the hell was going on. Scofield told Edgar to tell him, "If that son-of-a-bitch comes close to us again, then I'm going to blow him out of the sky." That pilot pulled about two to three hundred feet away from us and never came close again. When we landed, we figured their crew would want to start some kind of trouble with us, and we were so mad we would have cleaned their clocks. Luckily for them, they never said a word.

Henry Fishbone

To me, Fishbone, who was from East Orange, New Jersey, was the most courageous of us all. He was Jewish, and if we had been shot down over Germany, there was a damn good chance that he would have been sent to the mines as slave labor. We had been told that some flyers shot down over Germany were captured by farmers and pitchforked to death. Also, we had been told that some downed flyers were captured, had their hands tied, and were thrown into burning buildings. If shot down over

CHAPTER TWO

Germany, we had been instructed to surrender ourselves to a German soldier. If shot down over France, we were supposed to stay where we landed and wait for the French Underground to arrive. If shot down over Denmark, we were to find the nearest church and stay there for sanctuary. I wouldn't have gone into a church, though. After all, the Germans weren't stupid. But I would have found a church and stayed nearby.

On payday we always loved to hear Fishbone count his money because he had a way of snapping the bills so that you could hear it all over the hut. And whenever we were stationed at a field he would always put his name in to receive the town's daily paper. At one of the fields where we were stationed, he complained that every time he went to get his paper they didn't have any for him. We were all together one day walking by the PX and he decided to find out what was happening to his daily paper. We went in with him, only mildly curious but curious nevertheless. He told the girl behind the counter that his name was Fishbone and that he had signed up for the town paper but wasn't getting it. She said, "We have no one listed by the name of Fishbone." Fishbone shrugged and as we were walking away she yelled out, "Wait a minute, we do have someone here by the name of Fishface." For the next couple of months Fishbone paid for taking us in with him to that PX. We all called him "Fishface."

Apparently Fishbone had better luck with women than he had with us or the girl behind that counter. He told us the story of how he would go on his dad's fish route because he was in love with one of the girls who lived on the route. After a while the girl's mother caught on to Fishbone's affections and every time she smelled the fish, she would send her daughter out to do some chores. Despite the mother's efforts to the contrary, Fishbone ended up marrying this girl. She was an extremely beautiful Jewish girl with lovely features. She was also great fun to be around. In the meantime, Fishbone's father had gone into the kosher chicken business.

During the bomb run on our fourteenth mission, the target was a tank factory at Dusseldorf, in the Rohr Valley. Fishbone had opened the bomb bay doors and was kneeling, waiting for the bombs to be dropped. The flak was coming up at us but good. Suddenly, the small pipe which was in the bomb bay area, through which all of the hydraulic fluid flows, got hit and the fluid sprayed out uncontrollably. Not being a mechanic, Fishbone saw the fluid and immediately thought it was a flame. He shouted out, "Fire! Fire in the bomb bay!"

When I heard the word "fire," I threw myself backwards out of the turret, tore off my flak jacket, grabbed my parachute and hooked it to the harness. Stewart already had the escape hatch open. With our earphones still on, we were ready to jump. In the meantime, Pete had come down from his top turret and yelled over the intercom, "No fire! No fire! It's hydraulic fluid." What a relief! No one wants to bail out during a bomb run, especially when the flak is coming up at you. I got back in my turret after taking off my chute. Stewart closed the escape hatch.

But the drama wasn't over yet. The tail turret was absolutely saturated with hydraulic fluid. It was all over the gun sight, gun handles and me. I was soaked. I reported the situation to the crew: "Hey, I can't see through my gun sight, and visibility from the tail is poor, because I've got this hydraulic fluid all over me."

Edgar said to me, "Picardo, whatever you do, don't light up a cigarette. We would explode if you did."

I said, "How in the goddamn hell can I light up a cigarette when I give them all to you? Don't *you* light up!" It was a relief to get out of the flak, because with any kind of hit we probably would have exploded. On our way home we were very concerned. As we approached the base in England, we were informed that we were coming into a strong head wind. Because we had lost our hydraulic system, we manually cranked down the landing gear and the flaps. Fortunately, Edgar was a helluva pilot, and we made a good landing with no brakes and no problems. The second time our hydraulic system was shot out, our target was the submarine pens at Kiel, Germany, and again I was soaked in hydraulic fluid. Over England we were told there were no head winds at our air base. Near the cliffs of Dover there was a very long emergency landing strip, and we were ordered to land there. Waiting there for us was a C-47 with its crew and they flew us back to our bomb group. Oh boy, that hot shower sure felt good. As you'll discover, this would be just two in a long series of close calls.

In Salt Lake City, we attended lectures and seminars in order to prepare us for flying combat. There was a lot of work involved during the ten days we stayed in the city of the Great Salt Lake, but we did manage to get away once, to visit the focus of the city, the Mormon Tabernacle. What a place! It was quite a sight and dominated the area for miles around. But I must say the highlight of Salt Lake City wasn't the Mormon temple but Les Brown and his band. Doris Day was his vocalist— wearing a white dress with red polka dots she was so beautiful that she reminded us young men what we were fighting for.

McCook, Nebraska

I could never understand how, when stationed at a military base for a few weeks, GIs could end up getting married to some girl they had just met. To me, everything during the war was so uncertain. There simply wasn't enough time for a long-lasting relationship. As far as I was concerned, marriage was completely out of the question.

At McCook, Nebraska, I met a crazy, funny Italian man from Philadelphia named Alfonse. Like me, Al was loud and obnoxious. He was also small, and maybe that was why they made him the belly gunner on his crew. Both obnoxious Italian-Catholics, Al and I were natural friends. We understood each other implicitly.

Al's brother had been a tail gunner on a B-24 stationed in Australia. But while we were there, Al received a letter from his mother saying that his brother had been reported as missing in action. His squadron had bombed the Japanese base at Rabaul, a small island east of New Guinea. The letter was written in Italian, and he read it to me. The last line has always stuck with me: "You must have patience and courage, my son." I've never forgotten those words. She must have been a very strong person with great faith, especially since she knew that Al himself was flying on a B-24 and would soon be flying combat missions somewhere. I admired her very much.

When Al received the letter, he became extremely upset. The radio operator on his crew and I both tried to console him, but what can you say to someone who in all probability has lost his brother? It wasn't enough to say that if Al's brother had been lost at sea, our boys would be searching for him around the clock. I know no one could have said anything helpful to me if my brother had died in the war. Even in McCook, Nebraska, you couldn't escape the ravages of war.

One night we went into town to a USO dance. I always loved the big band sounds of USO dances and can still hear those tunes as clearly today as I did fifty years ago. That evening I was having a lot of fun, talking and dancing with the girls, when I noticed that Al wasn't anywhere to be seen. I looked for him for a while, but I finally decided that he must have returned to the base early because he was so upset about the loss of his brother.

But when I returned to the base, Al wasn't to be found anywhere. Almost immediately, I was worried, hoping he hadn't done anything drastic. That probably would have made things worse. In the morning Al's crew approached some of us about him. He still hadn't returned, and by then his pass had expired. Al's pilot checked the base jail as well as the hospital and, finally, the morgue. No Al anywhere, though we were all relieved that he hadn't ended up in the morgue.

We twiddled our thumbs all day long, thinking about Al. Finally, he showed up late in the afternoon. Luckily, the MPs at the gate didn't check his pass close enough to know that he was long overdue. When we met him, he smiled and told us that he had met not only the most beautiful girl in the world, but also the greatest listener in the world. Al had told her all about his brother. He had walked her home from the dance, and she had invited him in because her parents were out of town visiting some relatives.

The reason why he had been late getting into base was because when they woke up early in the morning she wouldn't let him leave until she was sure that none of the neighbors would see him. Finally, as the clock ticked into the afternoon, Al crawled across the backyard and climbed over the fence into the back alley.

From that point, whenever Al could, he headed back to town and his new love. We never went into town together anymore because he was altogether too occupied. One day, though, he told me that he was going to see the base chaplain to get permission to marry her. "She's so beautiful—she's everything I want in a woman," Al kept saying to anyone willing to listen.

Almost immediately, without ever having met this dream woman, I told Al he was crazy to think about marrying her. I tried to reason with him: "Why not wait until after the war to find a wife? You never know what might happen." Al just shook his head. "Wait until you meet her. Then you'll understand." I think the girl's parents agreed with me. They were very much against the marriage because they felt they hadn't had a chance really to know one another.

Despite my warnings to the contrary, Al and his girlfriend got married on the base by the chaplain. They had a small reception following the ceremony at a club near the base. It was there that I met her. What a sight! This poor girl was so ugly that if she had wanted a glass of water, she would have to sneak up on the glass. It's amazing what a war will do to you to change your vision of beauty. Al had divulged all of his emotions to this girl and as far as Al was concerned, she was beautiful. And, after all, what else matters? Shortly after the wedding, Al's crew was shipped to a base in Montana. The bride was to stay in McCook for the time being. And although he told me he would stay in touch with me, he never did. War is absolutely great for separating you from people you care about. I never heard from Al again.

I've often wondered over the last fifty years if Al had made it through the years with his wife? Was his brother ever found? For that matter, did Al survive the war? These are questions, I suspect, that will never be answered for me. I sure hope for Al's mother's sake that her boys returned safely. I still think about her stoic, absolute belief in God. I wish I had that kind of faith.

We had been sent to McCook to pick up our bomber and begin actual combat training. I told Edgar that I was willing to fly the tail, but he put me in the nose turret at the front of the plane. During our first training flight I forgot all about being a tail gunner. I wanted to be at the front of the action. I would look back at those four Pratt & Whitney engines and became instantly drunk with power. I felt like I stuck out in front of the bomber like a king. It was great. Edgar had put Scofield in the tail. But after our first flight up, Scofield made it clear that he wasn't ever going to fly the tail again. He didn't want any part of being at the back of the plane. So Stewart was assigned to the tail gunner position.

The next time up in the air, Stewart flew as tail gunner. But when we arrived back, Stewart said there was no way he was going back into the tail. It made him sick as a dog to be stuck back there. I stayed quiet, happy as a lark that I had been lucky enough to be in the nose even though I as good as volunteered for the tail.

The following day, I was sitting in the PX drinking a milk shake. Edgar came in, saw me and said, "Hey, Picardo." Before he could say another word I said, "I know, I'm your new tail gunner." He said, "That's right!" My days in the nose turret had been short-lived. We were to go up the next day to practice low level flying and strafing. I would never go into that plane again as anything other than a tail gunner.

When you're sitting in the tail turret you can't see any part of the airplane. You can only see where you've already been, not where you're going. On that first day I discovered that the air could be heavy when flying at low altitude, and when the air is heavy like that, it gets very

CHAPTER TWO

bumpy and you begin to feel like you're a sheet in the wind. As you might expect, I got airsick as hell. A couple of the crew members came to get me out of the turret and put me in the copilot's seat until I felt better. That happened a couple of times until I got used to the bumpy ride. I still missed the nose, but somebody had to fly the tail, and that somebody was me. I'll always think fondly of McCook, Nebraska, because it was in this little Midwestern town that I became a tail gunner.

Casper, Wyoming

We heard the day before we arrived in Casper that the army had kicked out 350 prostitutes from town so there would be housing available for the wives. Edgar, Fishbone and Scofield were all married, so their wives came to join them. Moskovitis sent for his girlfriend, and they were married there. Scofield was the best man in the wedding. The reception took place at the Riverside Restaurant, and I remembered the wedding reception in the ballroom of The Big House in Seattle. I felt like a member of a big family again. Because money was tight, the Scofields and the Moskovitises shared a tiny one bedroom apartment together. The bedroom was so small that they hung a bedsheet over a clothesline down the middle of the room so that they couldn't see each other's bed. I can just imagine what their wedding night was like. Oh, boy.

We continued our training in Casper with more formation flying and practice bomb runs. The pilots trained with flight simulators that taught them how to fly blind, only using instruments. Also practicing on simulators were the bombardier and the navigator, while the radio operator was attending radio school. We gunners spent all of our time learning how to track enemy fighters. After a few weeks of intensive training, we left Casper for Topeka, Kansas. This move must have been especially tough for the newlyweds, who had only spent about a month together. By contrast, I was fancy-free and determined to stay that way until the war was over.

Topeka, Kansas

One thing I thought I learned in Topeka was that I would never really be very comfortable with the B-24. Even though it flew like a dream, I thought the wings were too small for the size of the airplane. One day the pilot came to the crew and informed us that a storm was coming our way, and a weatherman in Topeka wanted to fly through the eye of the storm. He had asked Edgar if he was willing to do it. For some reason Edgar agreed, asking if any of the guys wanted to join him. I was interested and, as it turns out, so was everyone on our crew. I can't be certain just how many of us really wanted to do it, but we all went.

Maybe this gives a sense of just how much we all trusted Edgar, because we figured he would never take us somewhere unnecessarily that was dangerous. I think it also says something important about the camaraderie we developed during our time together. But maybe if I had known what the heck the eye of a storm is, I would have reconsidered. Well, I sure found out!

CHAPTER TWO

By the time we took off we could actually see the storm coming our way. On this flight I negotiated my way out of the tail, because I wanted to see what was coming, not what was going. In fact, I somehow managed to work myself up front and sat talking to the weatherman. I don't know why, but I hadn't strapped myself in. Suddenly, I felt like a ping pong ball being slammed between four walls. I figured I was a goner and that this was the end. I wouldn't be killed by a Luftwaffe fighter or a flak attack, but by a stupid storm that I had no business investigating, anyway. Finally, though, we flew out of the storm, and I had escaped with only a few bruises.

When we landed, we all departed from the plane rather gingerly. Edgar came up to us with a sheepish look on his face, maybe the only time I ever saw him look sheepish. He told us that in the middle of the storm he had completely lost control of the plane, and when he had finally regained it, he had said to himself, "I'll never do this again." The best thing that came from this experience was knowing that our bomber could stand up to the worst the elements could produce. From that day on, I had complete confidence in the B-24. I don't think they were built to fly through the eye of a storm, but they could if they had to.

One day our squadron was told to fly a simulated bombing mission. The target was the water tower at Omaha, Nebraska. We were also going to be "attacked" by P-47 fighter planes called Thunderbolts. We had cameras in our guns that would record our shooting accuracy. When we were attacked, every time we would pull the

141

trigger on our twin .50-caliber guns, the camera would take a picture. We thought we were prepared for the worst any P-47 could give us.

On our way to the target, the P-47s showed up and when we had them in our sights we started pulling our triggers like crazy. For all we knew, we believed that we had them dead in our sights. When we arrived at the target we dropped our "bombs" (more pictures) and headed home. As soon as we landed, the technical support people arrived and took away our guns in order to retrieve the cameras and develop the film. I figured that we had done a great job of defending ourselves against the "enemy" attack.

The next day the base commander called a meeting. When he began to speak he had a sarcastic tone in his voice, "I'm sure glad that I'm not going overseas with you guys to fly combat missions. Just take a look at these films." What we saw was both funny and disturbing. In the sights of our guns you could see just as many B-24s as you could see P-47s. We had been shooting at our own bombers! Talk about friendly fire. Geez.

So we went back to basics again, flying tight formations and practicing tracking fighter planes. A week later we were assigned the same mission, and were relentlessly attacked by P-47s. But when the film was developed this time, only P-47s were in the frame of the pictures. The commander was like a different man when he spoke to us about this. He said simply, "I think you guys are ready."

CHAPTER THREE
Tail Gunning

Off to War

By this time, we were preparing to be shipped overseas to a combat outfit. We were given our choice of where we wanted to go. I wanted badly to go to the South Pacific to fight the Japanese Empire. The copilot wanted to go to Italy. The other eight crew members all wanted to go to England and join the 8th Air Force. We had a working democracy, so England it was. I think the boys chose England because the living conditions there were supposed to be better than in other places during the war.

From Topeka, we flew on a brand new aircraft to Westover Field in Springfield, Massachusetts. We were to fly from there to England. On our way to Springfield, Edgar discovered that the airplane could climb on fewer RPMs than the engine was actually designed for. The bomber had been built at Willow Run by the Ford Motor Company. The company was notified of Edgar's discovery, and two engineers were sent out to find out how such a phenomenon was possible.

While the engineers were inspecting the plane, I met a guy who had been stationed in England, so I thought I might find something out about my new home. He informed me that the English woolen blankets we would be issued were extremely coarse and that all you had on your bunk was a mattress cover, pillow and blanket, with no sheets. So before I left for England, I stole a sheet and stuck it in with my belongings.

The engineers from Ford had us flying around Springfield trying to figure out what had caused the RPM difference. What I couldn't understand was why they didn't simply give us another plane and return this one back to the factory. But I was only a sergeant and didn't understand the bureaucratic technicalities of the war. Finally, the commander of the base put his foot down on all the testing and yelled, "Hey, D-Day! They're hitting the beaches at Normandy. Get your butts over to England, and get to work pounding the Germans!"

The two engineers never did determine why our plane could fly at such low RPMs but I guess they got a good Massachusetts vacation out of the deal. So we were off to Merrie Olde England from New England. It was June 6, 1944.

CHAPTER THREE

We took off from Westover Field in Springfield and headed over Bangor, Maine, and then to Labrador. The next day we flew to Iceland. We spent twenty-four hours there and it was daylight the entire time, which felt very strange to us. We gave the bomber a good looking over, a strict twenty-five-hour inspection. From Iceland, we flew to England, but the fog in East Anglia was so thick that we ended up landing in Wales. Two days later, we were flown to a school in Northern Ireland for more training.

Northern Ireland

We were informed that this would be the last ten days of education before our real education began in a bomber group that would regularly fly over the skies above France and Germany. These last ten days were serious business, they told us, and there would therefore be no passes. You should never tell a soldier, "No passes," when he's within walking distance from town.

One of my fellow crew members and I decided that we wanted to see what the nearest town looked like. We asked one of the GI's who had been there for a while what was the best way of getting into town without a pass. He told us to follow along the coastline, because patrols didn't go there very often. And that's what we did, leaving just a few minutes after he told us.

Less than a mile later, we were in town. Shortly after arriving, we heard some dance music coming from a nearby building, so we walked in and up the stairs. Here we discovered a lovely ballroom with a dance band and, more importantly, no MPs, though lots of bobbies stood around to provide security for the dance.

I was just standing there, surveying the scene, when a girl walked right up to me and asked if I was "just a buck." I said, "Yes, I'm a Buck Sergeant," and pointed to the stripes on my arm.

She said, "No, just a buck, just a buck," and started dancing.

I said, "Do you mean 'jitterbug?'" She nodded, smiled and pulled me onto the dance floor. I should have known right away that something was wrong with this girl, but I didn't really care because she was very pretty with big blue eyes, and very well built as well. We jitterbugged for quite a while. Finally, the music stopped and we found ourselves in front of the bandstand, and on the bandstand stood a photograph of King George.

My Irish beauty held my hand and walked me up to the photograph. I thought she was going to flatter her king, but was I in for a surprise. Instead, she looked at the picture and suddenly shouted, "You bastard!" and spit on it. Instantly, some guy threw a punch at her. I blocked it. A second later, someone hit me in the back of the head. The next thing I knew, I had bodies under me and bodies over me, and the guy I was with had me by one leg trying to remove me from the pile of mayhem. And there we were with no passes, in the middle of a political and religious firestorm between Catholics and Protestants. Catholic or not, it was a battle I wanted no part of. Luckily, the bobbies broke the fight up fast. Had they not intervened, they would have taken me out of there piece by piece. The bobbies escorted us out gently but firmly and asked that we please not come back. When we got back to the base nobody had even noticed that we were gone. I kept a memory of the night for quite a while though, because the back of my head was sure sore for several days. I was under the impression I was assigned to the 8th Air Force to fight the Germans, not the Irish.

Liverpool

After ten days of intensive training we were flown to Liverpool. There we picked up our bomber (B-24) and the rest of the crew. We were assigned to the 44th Bomb Group, nicknamed "Flying Eight Balls," a few miles north of Norwich by a small town called Shipdham. Arriving over our base, I noticed how pretty it was, surrounded by green grass and trees.

We were met by an officer who welcomed us to the base. But while the officer was talking to Spencer, his driver came over to us and asked, "Who's the tail gunner on this crew?" I told him I was. He said, "See that bomber over there?" pointing to a bullet-ridden plane on the runway. "It got a direct hit in the tail today, and they're sucking out what's left of the tail gunner."

Some welcome, I thought, but they're not going to do it to me!

The next day as we walked into the Groups Headquarters Building, we saw this big sign that read:

Good Morning! One more day closer to victory.

Oil Refineries and Frozen Butts

At morning briefings the commanders would detail for us the day's bombing target. Early on in the war, if the target looked like it would be intensely defended—like an oil refinery—some of the guys would get "sick" all of a sudden and refuse to fly. They were sick all right, but it had nothing to do with the flu. They were queasy because they figured there was a good chance they wouldn't be at the next morning briefing.

The most indispensable member of any crew was, of course, the pilot. On a bomber, the pilot was the absolute commander of the rest of the crew. Everyone must have confidence in him; otherwise, the crew's morale disappears. If a crew lost its pilot because of illness or injury, the crew would be grounded until he was well. If the pilot was lost, then the crew would fold, unless a veteran pilot could be found that the entire crew could agree to. If any of the rest of the crew was lost, volunteer replacements were found.

Before a crew flies a bombing mission, its pilot goes up for one mission as a guest observer with another bomber crew. When we first arrived at the 44th Bomb Group, Edgar had to perform his guest duty. You can imagine how we clamored around him on his safe return from the mission, asking him how it had been. Typically, Edgar was taciturn and reserved: "Oh, it was all right." Such an answer doesn't exactly inspire confidence. I didn't know what to think. Had I known how terrible a bombing mission could be, I might have put in for retirement right then and there. As it turned out, though, Edgar would fly thirty-five missions. Frank Collela, the copilot, Moskovitis, the top turret gunner, Stewart, the waist gunner, and Fishbone, the radio operator, all flew thirty-four missions. For reasons that will become clear soon, the bombardier and I each flew thirty-three missions. The navigator flew twenty-five missions and Scofield, the other waist gunner, flew twenty-one.

As the war progressed, the commanders made an important adjustment in terms of briefings. Instead of jumping right into describing the target and what level of resistance we could expect from it, they began by asking if anyone wasn't up to flying that day. This wasn't designed for airmen with already verified injuries or illnesses. If no one spoke up at that point, the doors would be locked and every airman in the room was flying, oil refinery or no oil refinery. I attended plenty of briefings where guys wished they had spoken up early rather than find out that they might be blown out of the sky. Hearing the words "oil refinery" come out of the mouths of the briefers was a harrowing experience. In fact, just writing those words still gives me butterflies.

On the day of a mission, we were awakened very early in the morning, while it was still dark outside. It was always a disorienting experience to be up that early, and we would dress ourselves, still half asleep. We had a small hut housing three crews. That was only about fifteen enlisted men. Some huts were a lot bigger, but I preferred the smaller ones. That way I got the chance to know and trust all the guys. I didn't want to be waking up in the middle of the God-forsaken morning and not know instinctively who I was up with. A few minutes after wake-up, a truck would come by and take us over to the mess hall for breakfast. After breakfast, we jumped into another truck that took us to the pre-mission briefing. It was there that we would meet our day's destiny. Too many American flyers learned at those briefings where they were going to die. Somehow my crew avoided that fate.

Because we flew daylight missions, we usually took off right after daybreak. The earliest I was ever up for a mission was 2:00 a.m. Pre-mission briefings lasted for about thirty minutes. First, the briefers would show us the target, then the route to the target. The color we didn't want to see on the target was red. The more red we saw, the more flak there would be. Next on the briefing list were the identification of nearby Luftwaffe airfields that might supply German fighters. It was also important to know how many gallons of gas we would carry, as well as what type of bombs we were going to drop.

The briefers told us the proper formation to line up in and then informed us whether we would be flying over the Channel or the North Sea. This depended on whether we were hitting a target in Germany or France. We learned the altitude we would be flying at, and the time we were scheduled to hit the enemy coast. Next came how much flak we could expect over the target. You better believe that the mention of flak got everyone's attention quickly. One of the most important parts of the briefing was finding out where we would meet our fighter escorts or as we called them, "our little friends," what kind of enemy fire we could expect as we started the bomb run, and where we would rendezvous with our escorts once the run was over. Finally, we were told what time we were expected back. This was also important, because all we were shooting for on the mission was to be back on English soil at that time. To do so meant we had flown a successful mission, and we were alive.

The B-24 could carry a ten-thousand-pound bomb load and up to twenty-seven hundred gallons of gas (the wings housed the gas tanks). With the crew, the .50-caliber machine guns, the ammunition and our personal equipment, a fully loaded B-24 was one heavy aircraft. On take-offs, I was the only one in back between the waist gunners' windows. The rest of the crew stayed in front, between the cockpit and the bomb bay section. The pilot and I stayed on the intercom together, and I would watch all four engines from the waist area to make sure all was in order mechanically.

Leaving our dispersal area, we would taxi to the main runway and wait for our turn to take off. When we turned and lined ourselves up in the main runway, the pilot would lock the brakes, pushing all four throttles full forward. Every part of the plane would shake. The first few times I went through this, I was certain we were cracking up before we even got into the air. Then I got used to it. At this point Edgar would release the brakes and slowly start to roll forward. We would pick up speed and then start bouncing before getting airborne. Sometimes the fuel mixture in some of the engines would be, as they said back then, "too rich." A flame would then be thrown out of the engine's exhaust. When I saw this, I would call out the engine number and the pilot would adjust the fuel mixture. If all went well, the engine would clean itself up. Sometimes it took so long to pick up a head of steam that we would be just a few feet off the ground at the end of the runway. We were always told that if anything went wrong it was safe to bail out once we reached eight hundred feet. I even knew some crew members who bailed out at six hundred feet and made a safe parachute landing.

Whenever we had a mission deep into Germany, like at the Berlin or Munich area, to bomb factories or oil refineries, we would carry twenty-seven hundred gallons of fuel topped off. That meant that when we finished warming up all four engines, the gas trucks would come by and refill our tanks. This is when takeoff could get nerve-wracking. One day, as we took off with a full tank and started to climb, our number two engine threw out a flame from its exhaust. The gas started seeping out of the gas cap. It was about one foot above the flame. On the intercom I said very quickly to the pilot, "Two." He cleared it right up. We had been one flaming foot from eternity.

CHAPTER THREE

Post-mission briefings were a lot better than pre-mission briefings. There was no tension in a post-mission briefing. Why should there be? We were alive and could expect to fly another day. I couldn't say that about a pre-mission briefing. Pre-mission briefings were about what information we could get from Intelligence that might save our lives; post-mission briefings were about what information we could provide Intelligence so we might save someone else's life.

On one of our bombing missions, the wing man on my left exploded from a direct hit. Just after the plane exploded, I saw two parachutes open up. Someone had somehow survived the explosion. I told the rest of the crew that it must have been the waist gunners, because they are the only ones who are usually not strapped in, and not trapped in turrets. Adding to my conviction was the fact that once over France, I saw a bomber from our squadron at five o'clock low. It also exploded from a direct hit. When a bomber explodes it's like a cigarette lighter that you try to light but won't. You see the flash of fire for an instant, and then the fire goes out. All that's left is smoke. When this plane exploded, all I saw were little pieces of debris. About four months later, we heard that the two waist gunners from this bomber were back in England, thanks to the heroics of the French Underground. The American and Allied fliers had a lot of respect for the Underground because it performed many good works. When we found out about the two waist gunner survivors, we were informed that they would be shipped back to the States after their arrival because they knew too much about the French Underground, and they didn't want these GIs flying missions over France and Germany again.

When I heard about the survivors I just couldn't believe it. I kept saying that I had seen the plane explode with my own eyes. I hadn't seen any parachutes. I wondered what it would be like to have your bomber explode twenty-two thousand feet in the air and live to tell about it. I waited for their arrival, because I had to hear it from them to believe it. I figured this was the closest thing to a miracle that I was ever going to see. When I finally saw them, I touched them and asked, "What was it like?" They said it was like being hit hard in the back of the head. They figured they both came to at about five thousand feet and pulled their rip cords. Their chutes opened without a problem. When they hit the ground, one of the gunners broke his leg. Other than that, they were fine. They said the French Underground took damn good care of them. But that's all they could tell us about the Underground.

Had we ever been shot down over France and picked up by the Underground, we had been ordered to do whatever we were told. Our commanders told us that if we were asked to slap a German officer in the face, we had to do it, no questions asked. If a member of the Underground was ever caught, he or she was tortured unmercifully and usually killed. The Germans would do anything to get them to talk. If caught, we would only end up in a POW camp. That was a pretty significant difference.

CHAPTER THREE

I don't know how to explain the enormous feeling of relief that accompanies returning safe from a bombing mission. I'm afraid you would have to live through it to know it and I wouldn't wish that on my worst enemy if he didn't want to go up in a bomber. Once on the ground, you started to live for the future again and plan what you might do once the war was finally over. It was like being granted a reprieve from a death sentence. I was filled with hope that I would see the Seattle Rainiers again, as well as my family and friends. I've never had a feeling to compare with it, before or since.

We would know by late afternoon or early evening if the group was flying the next day and, on top of that, if our crew had been picked for the mission. If we were picked, that night I would say five decades of the rosary and then try my best to forget about the mission. It didn't do any good to worry. It sure didn't improve your chance of coming back—at least not like the rosary did. I remembered what my grandmother had told me: "If you pray, everything will be all right." I only took Grandmother's admonishment to heart on the night before flying, though. Other nights I just went to sleep. I'm glad God didn't count against me for it.

As a Catholic, after pre-mission briefings I would go into a small room with the rest of the Catholics, and we would meet with a priest there. This was true of fliers from other faiths as well. There was a Jewish room with a rabbi and a Protestant room with a minister. In a way, this is what we were fighting for against the Nazis:

the freedom to worship as we saw fit, and equal opportunity for everyone, regardless of ethnicity, religion or race. Catholics always received holy communion and the last sacraments. The priest would deliver the "Our Father" prayer and also a short prayer asking for God's special protection for us on the mission. After this, we would leave the room and get our parachutes.

I don't know if there was a connection between parachutes and what the priest said, but if given the choice today I might pick a parachute over a priest. It could have been a toss-up, though. One time, a wise guy handing out parachutes said to me as he gave me one, "If it doesn't open up, bring it back and I'll give you another one." This didn't make me feel too good, and I was extra glad I had said my rosary the night before. Priests were fine, but the rosary was Grandma's medicine and I was more than willing to take it.

After getting our parachutes we would jump back on a truck for the third time and the truck would take us to our bomber. Everyone would carefully check out his own equipment on the plane where our individual positions were. We all depended on all the other guys to make sure that the plane was totally prepared and safe. One careless inspection from any of us could have meant the difference between life or death. I went over that tail turret with a fine tooth comb.

Then, depending on the weather, we would either get in the plane or hang around it, waiting for the flare to be fired, signaling us to start our engines. People always ask me if everyone was quiet and somber prior to take off. But that wasn't the way it was at all, at least with our crew. Everyone always cracked jokes at that time of the day, probably to break up the tension. Time seemed to stand still while we waited in our dispersal area, so when the final flare went up, we felt like we were on our way.

Once, the bombardier and I got frost-bitten and we were grounded for one mission while we healed. I had gotten frostbite when my oxygen mask tube froze. I wasn't getting any oxygen, so I had to unhook the tube, break up the ice and then reattach the tube. Unfortunately, some of the ice that I broke up in the tube spilled on my cheek and neck, and by the time we arrived back in England, I had suffered such a bad case of facial frostbite that I couldn't put on my oxygen mask.

The morning of the mission, I got up with the rest of the crew and ate breakfast with them. I wished them all good luck then returned to the hut for more sleep. A few hours later, the bombardier came by and woke me up, "Hey, I want someone to talk to. I wonder how the guys are making out? They were supposed to be over the target at nine-fifty-five, and they should be well on their way back by now, because it's eleven-thirty."

I couldn't believe what time it was already, "Boy," I said, "did I sleep that long?" The bombardier and I wondered out loud what life would be like if our crew didn't return. We both started to sweat this one out.

We went to the mess hall together to get some coffee, but we couldn't do anything else except wait and wait.

All of a sudden we heard the distinctive sound of P-51s buzzing our field. We knew then that the 44th Bomb Group was over England. The only question we had was if our plane and crew were among them. We jumped on our bicycles and pumped them to the landing field. It wasn't long before we heard the roar of the engines overhead and a few moments later we started to make out the planes in the sky. We knew that thirty-six bombers had taken off, so we started counting. We spotted thirty-one. What followed were the yellow flares, indicating wounded aboard some of the planes. They landed first. Then the remaining bombers started peeling off one by one, coming in for their landings. Finally, we spotted the St. Christopher. There weren't any yellow or red flares either. Great, they had made it back in good shape.

We met them at the Red Cross truck. Abercrombie, who flew the tail that day, said to me, "How in the hell do you fit in that thing? Half of me felt like it was outside the turret. I don't like it. You can have it."

Stewart then chimed in with his two bits, "It was a pleasure to fly a mission without hearing your howling, which you claim is singing."

I told him he was just jealous he didn't have a voice like Sinatra. "When I'm famous there won't be any free concert tickets for you."

Pete added, "It <u>was</u> quiet without you up there." When Pete spoke, it finally dawned on me. It was then I realized I had just made the biggest mistake of my tail gunner career. I had completely forgotten about Pete's

---

bottle of Fitch Shampoo filled with booze. That bottle and I had been in the hut all alone together for hours. I could have gotten a small container to pour a few shots into for future use.

Pete's ribbing was characteristic of our crew. We were extremely close, as you might expect of a group of men who entrusted their lives to each other's hands almost daily. No one story or anecdote can convey our affection for one another. If you needed a few bucks until payday, someone was always there to lend it to you. I believe you can measure someone's character by the degree to which you can trust them in a life and death situation, and by this criteria the men in my crew were some of the best people ever assembled.

We played a lot of poker (personally, pinochle was my favorite game). Poker was appropriate, since we were betting against our lives every time we went up in the air. A little game of poker didn't amount to a hill of beans compared to those stakes. Sometimes we would play with members of different crews. It wasn't unusual to have enjoyed a game of cards with another crew so much that we would want to strike up another game a few days later. Often, though, they just weren't around anymore. Strangely, it might not have really hit us that they were gone until we wanted to play cards with them.

None of us really excelled as card players, but it was a good way to pass the time. We would also go to movies shown on the base and attend base dances. If we didn't have a date for a dance we might hit the stag line or just sit there and listen to the band play what we called the "big band sound." Today you might consider this good old fashioned dance music, but in my day it was the most modern music around. When we weren't jitterbugging, we held our partners close, sometimes dancing cheek to cheek. We held her close because we didn't know if this might be the last time we would ever be so lucky to have a woman in our arms.

In addition to playing cards and going to dances, our crew enjoyed just sitting around and talking to one another, making fun of one another. Everyone's sense of humor was great. Of the crew, Pete Moskovitis and George Scofield made me laugh the most. Laughter was an important antidote to the possibility of death. Going to our club on the base was also a lot of fun. We played pool and drank beer, sometimes to excess but not often. I truly can't remember any of the crew getting mad at one another. To be sure, we teased each other unmercifully, but everyone gave as good as they got. We liked each other so much that when we showered we would wash the other guy's backs. It felt great.

When we showered, we would also wash our clothes at the same time. Washing and drying clothes (especially drying in rainy England) took up a lot of time. If the weather was good, we would hang our clothes on the line. Sometimes my sheet would take all day to dry—other times we would give up on outside drying and dry our clothes instead on the small stove in the hut.

The day the bombardier and I had off from flying wasn't like a normal day out. On normal days off when we had flown the day before, we would be so tired that we couldn't do much of anything. As a rule, we would clean our bunks and the area around them, sew our socks, and wash clothes. If the weather was good, we would play baseball, but more often we would stay inside and play cards. This was, after all, England, and good weather didn't happen very often. The weather off the coast of the North Sea changes so fast you can't believe it. Sometimes you will wake up in the morning and see a brilliant sunrise. And then an hour later all you can see are clouds. Every imaginable weather system blows in and out of that island kingdom in a twenty-four hour period. It wasn't the most dependable place for baseball—maybe even less dependable than rainy Seattle.

If you can believe it, sometimes we would have to take a refresher class for a couple of hours in some aspect of flying. Then there were times where we would get a bunch of airmen together and go to S2—Intelligence. S2 would brief us on what was going on all the war fronts around the world. That was always interesting, especially because it seemed like we were really beginning to win the war handily. It didn't seem likely that either the Germans or Japanese could repel Allied advances much longer.

There were also times when we took the trucks into Norwich and spent some time there. Norwich wasn't (and still isn't) a very big town, but it at least offered us the diversions of something like city life. If we didn't have the whole day to spend, or didn't have the use of a truck, we would jump on our heavy black 1940s bicycles and pedal over to the pub, which was about a quarter of a mile from the airfield. Pub life was always fun when you were with a bunch of crazy guys. And chances were, if you were with Army flyers, they were all crazy. Only rarely did we ever fly again the day immediately after a mission. That could be tough, because any mission, whether it was an oil refinery or an easier target, was absolutely exhausting. But if a target was ready to be hit, we went. The commanders tried to give us at least one day off between missions, but they couldn't guarantee us anything. Sometimes two or even three days would go by before we would fly again. The weather was always a big factor in this decision. In England the fog could set in indefinitely and ground us for days.

As a tail gunner, I always had to stay active in back of the plane. Tail gunners were trained always to keep their turrets and guns moving. This was meant to signal enemy fighters that we were alive and well, and if they came in our direction they could expect a brawl.

One of my worst flying experiences occurred while we were bombing an oil refinery in Hanover, Germany. As usual, encountering oil refinery flak was so thick, it was like flying through a cloud of shrapnel and bullets. It was a tail gunner's version of hell, because he is so vulnerable and exposed at the back of the plane. I was looking out for any German planes while we rode through the flak. Flying through flak to get to a bomber was a very dangerous thing for a fighter to attempt, but as the war progressed and the Germans became more desperate, they had been known to do so. Suddenly, a shell exploded under the tail turret, making an enormous "BANG!" The ensuing concussion slammed me half out of the turret, then threw me forward against the gun handles and knocked the wind out of me.

For a few moments I thought we had exploded. If we had, there wasn't anything I could do about it, because we would lose altitude so fast there wouldn't be time to bail out. I covered my eyes with both arms because I didn't want to see the ground zooming toward me. In those days the elevators were so fast and abrupt that when you went up, you had to wait a few seconds for your stomach to join you. I had heard the same thing happened to an airman when a plane went down. Thank God I didn't get that sensation then!

I pulled my arms from my eyes and saw that we were still in formation. What a great feeling that was! The intercom had been silent for a while but it suddenly crackled on and I heard the pilot call back to one of the waist gunners, "Go and see what's left of Picardo."

Before the waist gunner had time to move I was shouting into the intercom, "What do you mean what's left of Picardo? I'm fine." Later I learned that they thought we had received a direct hit in the tail because the concussion had knocked the controls out of the copilot's hands. That was the same mission I saw our wing man on my left explode. I saw no chutes open. Earlier that morning, their nose gunner, Jim, had sat across from me at breakfast. Now he was gone.

We always wore flak suits on those missions. Coming back I was tired and leaned forward, sticking my butt out the back end of the turret. I didn't think anything of it because I was wearing a heated suit. I don't know how long I was in that position, but probably for at least two hours. As we approached our air base for landing, I tried to sit straight only to discover that my butt burned so badly I couldn't even think about putting any weight on it. When we landed the tail section looked like a sieve, there were so many holes in it. On the right side behind the tail turret there was a hole big enough to put a basketball through. On the opposite side there was a hole large enough to throw a football through, even if you weren't much of a quarterback. My butt had stuck out in such a way that it was in the crosswind of the two holes. Both cheeks were frostbitten. I never thought this could happen wearing a heated suit, but I'm here to tell you that it can.

I was taken to the medics—and boy did they get a kick out of a frostbitten butt! I had never realized until then just how dangerous bombing an oil refinery was. I soaked both cheeks in lukewarm water, and later they put some kind of salve on the afflicted area. Slowly I began to feel it again. Two days later I was flying again. It's unbelievable that with all of those holes in the tail section I hadn't received a scratch. I didn't ever see any guardian angels in the war, but I must have had at least one. But I would have liked to complain to him about letting me fall prey to a frostbitten butt.

CHAPTER THREE

For Uncle Joe

We were awakened early one morning, being one of nine crews from the 67th Bomb Squadron scheduled to fly a bombing mission. We hurried and dressed, the truck came by and picked us up, and we headed for breakfast in the mess hall. At the briefing that morning, we learned the target was the oil refinery at Magdeburg, Germany. We were told the oil from this refinery was being shipped to the German troops on the Russian Front. They wanted this refinery leveled. Uncle Joe had requested it. I asked one of my crew members, "Who the hell is Uncle Joe?"

"Joseph Stalin, you idiot!" he replied.

After the briefing and receiving of Holy Communion, I went to a room where I left my wallet and other personal things. I picked up my chute, jumped in a jeep and headed for our aircraft. I was the first one there. When I arrived, I noticed a captain standing by the plane. He was a paratrooper. I was looking him over, but we didn't say a word to one another. I noticed he had his chute, a backpack, a pistol in his holster, a dagger in its case next to the holster, and he was carrying a carbine rifle. He looked like he was going camping. Finally I spoke up and said, "Captain, you know we're coming back."

He said, "Oh, I knew that."

The rest of my crew arrived and he introduced himself to our pilot, Spencer. He was coming along.

Our bomb group flew in three squadrons, twelve bombers in each squadron: the lead squadron, our high right and then our low left squadron. The lead squadron had its pilot in the lead plane which led the whole group, with his deputy lead flying off of its right wing. Heading east and finally reaching the enemy coast, our lead plane developed mechanical problems with one of its engines. It was losing oil pressure fast, so the pilot turned off the engine and feathered the prop, banked out of formation and headed back to England.

Our deputy lead was now our lead plane, and we became the deputy lead. We were on course. About an hour and a half later, we neared the target. On reaching our IP, we turned, opened our bomb bay doors and started our bomb run. The flak started coming up hot and heavy. Our lead plane's number three engine got hit and caught fire. They released their bombs, banked and got out of the formation. They never got back to our base, and we never saw them again.

Our crew took over the lead. Crean, our bombardier, took control of the bomb run. When he dropped his bombs, the rest of the group dropped theirs. Banking and getting out of the target area, I could see the target covered with smoke through the flak. Looked like a good hit. Our navigator, John, set his course, and the group was on its way home. We met our fighter escort and headed west.

Finally, landing at our base, we got into a truck and headed for the Red Cross van for coffee and donuts.

CHAPTER THREE

The paratrooper told Spencer that he had always wanted to go on a bombing mission. When he talked to Colonel Snavley, the Group Commander, he had told him, "I want to fly with the best crew you've got." Snavley recommended Spencer. "I don't know if you are the best crew," the paratrooper said, "but you have to be the screwiest."

Maybe he said that because, kiddingly, I had told the bombardier on the way over, "For a change, let's try to drop our bombs inside of Germany."

"Ya, ya, ya," he had answered,

The paratrooper then picked up his equipment, walked away, and we never saw him again. We just looked at one another and shrugged. It was just another day in the sky over Germany. I was tired. We had taken a beating and lost some bombers. Sitting at the briefing table a voice behind me asked, "Who's the tail gunner on Spencer's crew?" Being the tail gunner in the lead plane in the lead squadron, I was the only one who could see every bomber in the formation. Without looking back I said, "Me."

I was asked, "What did you think of the formation?"

I yelled out, "Piss poor!!" When I looked back, I saw it was General Leon Johnson. It was the first time I had ever even seen a General. This man had been awarded the Congressional Medal of Honor. I looked at Spencer, whose eyes were almost popping out of his head.

The General asked again, "What did you think of the day's formation?"

I told him a revised version: "It was sloppy and well spread out."

He said, "Thank you, Sergeant, that's all I wanted to know."

When he left, Spencer growled, "You don't talk to a general like that."

"I didn't know I was talking to a general," I told him.

But I didn't get to tell the general how proud I was of our navigator and bombardier. I thought they deserved a medal for taking over and doing so well.

Glenn Miller

In August of 1944, the 44th Bomber Group flew its two hundredth bombing mission. They gave us a day off to celebrate.

The Glenn Miller Army Air Corps Band was there, and that caused excitement. There was a rumor that Princess Elizabeth was going to be there. She was known to visit military bases around the British Isles. I had seen her picture in the local newspapers and thought she was kinda cute.

We were in our hut talking about her. Someone asked, "Would you marry her, if you were given the chance?"

Some idiot spoke up: "Sure, I'd marry her. I would love to be a king!" He was informed that he would not become a king. Lucky for the Princess, her visit was just a rumor.

The Miller bandstand was set up in a hangar, to hold the huge audience of both GIs and civilians who lived in the area. I had to sit so far away that the musicians looked like they were an inch tall. But I loved the band music and singing. The last piece they performed was the U.S. Army Air Corps song. To this day, I still remember the ending lyrics:

Up in Fame or down in flames,
Nothing can stop the Army Air Corps.

Memorable Missions

Once when we were on our way to a target in southeastern Germany, we were flying right alongside the white capped Alps, and they seemed so close we could touch them. As it turned out, they would be the second most beautiful thing I would ever see.

In the middle of my Alps reverie, all of a sudden Pete called me over the intercom, "Hey Ed, have you seen any of our fighter support?"

Stunned for a second, I cried, "No!" This was strange. There weren't any P-51s around, as the pre-mission briefing had indicated there would be. As airmen, this made us feel very uneasy, especially when no one on the crew had seen hide nor hair of them. Boy, was I looking out for them after that. A few moments later, the copilot, Frank Collela, let everyone know what he'd heard over his radio, which was turned into the group's activity, not the crew. Frank called out, "Bandits in the area!" These were words we never enjoyed hearing. I sighed and sat up and, if it was possible, started concentrating even more than I had before. I knew I had to provide extra focus on protecting the back of the plane, or we might never have a view of the Alps again.

I was remembering what happened to the 445th when they missed their fighter support. Their gunners had .50-caliber machine guns, but they might as well have been armed with slingshots when they came up against the German fighters and their nose section cannons. If we got one cannon shell in our wing gas tank, we would be history. I wished that we had cannons too, but it would have been even more impossible to hit them with cannon shells.

I remembered that day the 445th nearly met extinction, September 27, 1944, when our mission was to bomb the Henschel engine plant at Kassel, Germany. We, the 44th Bomb Group, were the last group in the formation. In front of us was the 445th Bomb Group. But their head navigator made a huge miscalculation. When the 445th hit the IP, they didn't turn and start their bomb run on Kassel. They just kept heading east, deeper into enemy territory. When we turned, started our bomb run and opened our bomb bay doors, I noticed the 445th was still heading east and muttered to myself, "Hey, what's the matter with you guys? The target is this way!"

I realized their fighter escort would be waiting for them after they dropped their bombs at Kassel. All of a sudden the flak came up hot and heavy. I forgot all about the 445th—we were being hit. On each mission my courage was tested, and without realizing it, I was working to keep my fear under control.

CHAPTER THREE

The next day we were told that the Germans had blown twenty and twenty-three millimeter cannon shells into the American bombers. With three minutes of air superiority over the 445th, the German fighters had shot down thirty of its thirty-seven bombers, before American fighter support finally arrived. Thirty bombers in three minutes adds up to a lost bomber every six seconds, or ten bombers a minute. The 445th did manage to shoot down some enemy aircraft.

These were not good statistics to be reciting to myself at the moment as we flew alongside the Alps, but I couldn't help it. "Brace yourself," I thought, moving my turret from left to right and my gun up and down. There wasn't a cloud in the sky, so when the Bandits arrived, we would know it. From the tail, I spotted the Bandits first. They were directly in front of me at five o'clock level. They were so much faster than us that they just dove through the formation, firing their cannons. All I could do was open fire and aim the best I could with my tracers. Still, I figured lots of us were done for. Where the hell were those escorts! We weren't very far from becoming a statistic.

Looking around, I didn't see any of our bombers going down. When the second wave hit us, I opened fire. I saw one of my tracer bullets bounce off the engine cowling of a Folke Wolfe 190. Talk about armor protecting your engine—Geez!

At four o'clock low, I saw one of our bombers explode. Another at seven o'clock high seemed to just split down the middle and break up. I saw no parachutes from either bomber. But I said to myself, "We are not going to be next!"

Then a certifiable miracle happened. Between the peaks of the Alps, directly over my turret, I saw one beautiful silver P-38 after another fly over me. I was so happy, I was waving at them. What a sight! The Alps had been gorgeous, but the P-38s topped them, still the most beautiful thing I've ever seen in my life. Without their arrival, I don't see how I would be around today to write this.

I assumed these P-38s came up from Italy to help us out, but I really don't know. Years later, I learned that the Hughes Aircraft Company had built some of those P-38s. Thanks, Howard, wherever you are.

Lord HawHaw

William Joyce, an Englishman and member of the British Fascist Party, gained notoriety in the summer of 1939 when he left England for Germany and was given immediate naturalization by Doctor Goebbels. He became an active voice in the German Propaganda Organization and was known by the name of "Lord HawHaw."

We'd hear him every afternoon on our American Armed Forces radio station. He'd always start with, "Germany calling, Germany calling." Then he'd tell us that once again the 8th had missed their targets and hit schools and hospitals instead. We'd thought that was strange as

S2 had told us some of the Luftwaffe generals were amazed at our accuracy.

He'd go on to say what fools we were for fighting a war so far from home where the F-4s, draft dodgers and factory workers were sleeping with our wives and sweethearts. This did bother some of the guys.

Early one morning we were waiting near our bombers for the green flares to go off which signaled to us to start our engines. Our target was the ammunition factory at Bonn, Germany. All of a sudden we saw red flares going up instead of the green which meant that the mission had been canceled.

That afternoon we were playing poker in our hut and, as usual, had the radio on. We heard the famous, "Germany calling" and Lord HawHaw started his broadcast. I was startled when I heard him say, "We were waiting for you today at Bonn!" This was the one and only time I can remember this happening.

We stared in amazement at each other.

When the war ended, he was captured and executed by the British Government.

Trouble at Karlsruhe

During one morning briefing, we learned the day's target would be the marshalling yards at Karlsruhe, in southeast Germany. Intelligence informed us that the rail yard was absolutely packed with heavy equipment that was ready to move out. That heavy equipment represented high numbers of Allied soldiers, either saved or lost.

For this mission, our bombers were armed to the hilt. The bombers from the 44th Bomb Group carried four two-thousand-pound bombs each, while other groups carried incendiary or delayed action bombs. Delayed action bombs were particularly effective, because they exploded hours and sometimes even days after falling, thereby keeping the enemy from removing equipment from the area and thus buying time for more bombing runs later in the week, if needed.

As we approached Karlsruhe, everything appeared like it was going according to plan. Our fighter support was excellent, and even though flak over the target was fairly heavy, it didn't seem like this was going to be a particularly dangerous mission. After all, it was nowhere near as bad as hitting an oil refinery. But as we reached our target, only two bombs were successfully released. Somehow the bomb shackles of the other two bombs had frozen and wouldn't release to wreak their destruction on the railyard of Karlsruhe. Without any hesitation, we pulled out of regular bomber formation with the bomb bay doors wide open and maneuvered in between the bomber formation and fighter support. We were heading south, towards France.

The bombardier, the one whose name was Crean and who lived on Pitkin Avenue in Somewhere, New York, was almost always smiling. But I doubt if he was smiling during this episode. His one-man parade was definitely in jeopardy of going up in smoke if those bombs weren't released.

CHAPTER THREE

In the meantime, the waist gunners were working feverishly to get those bombs to release. In those days, the "rules" of war, such as they were, prevented us from dropping live bombs on an occupied country, if the bomb wasn't dropping on a target. This was intended to protect the victims of an invasion, such as the French.

All of a sudden, the navigator yelled, "Hey, you guys, release those bombs!" In six short seconds we were going to be over France. Just at that instant, one of the bombs released. The waist gunners yelled at me, "Hey, Picardo, keep an eye on it!" As if I could keep my eye on a bomb dropped at twenty-two thousand feet. But I kept my eye peeled on the area where I thought it might hit. We closed the bomb bay door and managed to defuse the other bomb. All of a sudden I saw a huge flash and black, billowing smoke coming straight up at us. In a matter of a minute or so it had, amazingly, already caught up to our altitude. We returned to formation and headed home. A little while later we reached the spot over the English Channel where it was possible to drop our unused bombs. But the bomb still would not release, so we proceeded back to England.

On the days that our crew didn't fly and the bombing group was on a mission, some time during the late morning or early afternoon the P-51s would buzz over the fields. That signified that our bomb group had completed its mission and they were over England. Everybody who wasn't on duty, including civilians who worked on the base, would rush to the field either by foot or bicycle to welcome the bombers back in.

First you would listen for the roar of the engines overhead, then after you began to see them you started counting. You also looked for flares. Yellow flares meant there was a wounded airman, and these planes would come in first. Red flares meant that a plane was in trouble, and these would land next. It would take a good half hour to land all the planes because they would peel off three at a time.

On the return leg of our mission from Karlsruhe, here we came with a two-thousand-pound unexploded bomb which we knew to be defused. And we were the absolute last plane to land. The tower understood that we had the bomb aboard, but the people watching the landings didn't have any idea. As soon as we touched down, the shackle holding the bomb broke as a result of the jarring of the wheels on the runway. I watched the bomb hit the runway and go bouncing down along the way like a bowling ball from hell rolling down a lane. When the spectators saw this horrific sight, they started to scatter far and wide, falling over one another on their bicycles in a certified panic mode. It was hilarious to watch, but only because we knew everyone was perfectly safe as long as they didn't trample one another to death. By the looks of the bedlam on that runway, this was a distinct possibility.

When we attended the mission debriefing headed by S2 intelligence, the navigator explained how we had dropped the third bomb and how I had seen an eruption of black smoke ensue a few moments later. The navigator remembered our air coordinates precisely and related them to intelligence. At this juncture another S2 officer was called in and began talking to the navigator in a nearby room. Two days later, we were informed that we had accidentally hit a crude oil storage plant and that a day after the mission a group of P-38s and P-47s had been sent to dive bomb the whole area, destroying all the oil that was there. Talk about the fortunes of war! There's no way today's sophisticated military satellites could have located that target any better than we did. Talk about hitting the jackpot.

Helen

When we would return from a bombing mission, we landed, taxied the B-24 into its dispersal area and then took a ride to the debriefing in the trucks and jeeps designated to pick us up. The debriefing boys wanted to know everything that happened during a mission, especially what all the crew members had seen in terms of targets being hit. If they concluded that we had missed our target, you could bet that we would revisit it sooner or later.

One shy young English girl who volunteered for the Red Cross by serving coffee and doughnuts caught my eye every time I saw her. I would always try to kid her, to see if I could make her laugh. But it was tough, because there were so many guys around, and they wanted to talk to English girls, too.

One day when I wasn't flying, I spotted the Red Cross van waiting for that day's bombers to return from their mission. I figured the cute English girl would be there, so I strolled over. It didn't take me long to single her out and start up a conversation with her. She was very shy and neat, and did her work well. When I asked her a question or just talked to her, she would answer with two or three words and not pick up on the questions. She seemed to be a loner. To be sure, she came to the base alone and left alone. I wanted to see if I could get her to smile, laugh and talk. Despite her only answering in the shortest possible phrases, I learned that she lived about a mile from the base and that her name was Helen. She told me that she enjoyed coming to the base, helping as much as she could with the war cause.

Helen intrigued me. I really don't know why she first attracted me because she was a very plain girl, but she had a nice figure. She must have been about five-foot-three with a slender build and dark blonde hair. I asked her if she had a boyfriend. She turned red and said no. To make her feel better, I said, "I can't imagine anyone as pretty as you without a boyfriend." By this time I had started thinking she *was* pretty. "I wonder why you don't come to the base dances on Wednesday nights."

She replied, "I don't have anyone to go with, and I don't want to attend the dances alone."

Those base dances were great fun, a wonderful diversion from the war and the threat of death that was always in the back of every airman's mind. The big dance bands played at the dances, but just listening to the music was usually good enough for me. I enjoyed singing the popular songs of the day, like "Green Eyes," "Tangerine," and "That Old Black Magic." Sometimes returning from bombing missions, when we were safely beyond the range of German anti-aircraft guns, I would start singing. Believe me, my singing went over with the guys like a lead balloon. The whole crew would usually ride me unmercifully, informing me I had a voice like a foghorn. One of them even told me that if I had to sing, I should step out of the plane first. I also would sing in our hut sometimes, but I guess I was pretty bad, because I never got any applause, only a barrage of shoes.

Anyway, I told Helen that if she would attend the dance on the coming Wednesday that I would meet her there and make sure that she got home safely. We both had bicycles, which was the only means of transportation for most of us. I was surprised and delighted when she agreed to go with me.

At these dances we always had tag dancing. When the music would start and a guy had his eye on a girl, he would invite her to dance. After a little while, though, another guy would come up from behind and tag him on the shoulder. At that point the first guy had to give up his girl. If you were dancing with a pretty girl like Helen, sometimes even after just five or six steps, you had to surrender her to some other GI. This I didn't like so much, especially the night Helen came, because I had gone out on a limb to ask her myself. Let those other guys get their own date! Unfortunately, the tag rules applied just as much to Helen and me as anyone else, so I didn't see her too much when the dancing was going on. Even though a fair number of English girls would come on Wednesdays, there were always more guys than girls.

During intermission Helen and I sat and talked, enjoying the punch and cookies together. There wasn't any booze, of course, but before the dances some of the guys would sneak off to our club on base and have a few beers. Me, I would have a couple of shots of whiskey, thanks to the shampoo bottle sent by Pete's wife. I always felt pretty good before showing up at the dances.

The night Helen met me, she told me she wanted to do more than just volunteer for the Red Cross. She wanted to join the service, to serve her country and maybe see some of the world in the bargain. It was plain from the start that this was going to be a strictly platonic relationship. We just seemed to enjoy each other's company —there was no question of sex. Talking to Helen was somehow like talking to one of my sisters. She was the only girl in England I ever told that I was from Seattle and not North Hollywood. After the dance, we bicycled together to her house in the country. She lived on a small hay farm.

I met Helen again at the Red Cross van after the next bombing mission. She asked me if I had been scared. Like usual, I told her the truth, "You bet, Helen." I met her again at a dance a couple of weeks later. She was terrific company, and even though we never got involved with one another, we always had a good time together.

CHAPTER THREE

One day when no one else was around, an opportunity cropped up to swipe some sugar from the mess hall. For some reason, I immediately thought of Helen because I knew that civilians had very little sugar. The English were much more deprived during the war than Americans. So, being a good Catholic boy, I didn't think twice about it. I stole enough sugar to fill an empty cigarette carton.

As soon as I had some free time, I took my carton of sugar and biked it over to where Helen lived. I knew it wouldn't be a good idea to hand it to her at the Red Cross van. On arriving at the farm, I knocked on the door and waited. Finally, the door opened and there stood one big, stupid looking farmer.

I asked, "Is Helen home? I brought this for her."

He muttered, "No, she isn't home." While grabbing my carton of sugar, he thundered, "Get off of my property, Yank. If you've got a home, go to it!" He slammed the door right in my face. You're welcome for the sugar, I muttered. It was no secret that many of the British didn't like us, even though we were helping win the war for them. After all, the British were in a helluva more dangerous situation with Hitler than the Americans were. I think they probably needed us more than we needed them, but they were terrific fighters, our most loyal allies before and after the war.

Once I left the hay farm and started riding back to the base on my bicycle, I started laughing to myself, because I realized that stupid jackass must have thought that there were cigarettes in the carton. Why wouldn't he?! The English loved American cigarettes much more than their own. He must have been terrifically disappointed to open up the carton, only to discover sugar. I hope he had a sweet tooth!

When I met Helen at the dance the following Wednesday, I told her that I had dropped by to see her but that she hadn't been home. She said that she had gone to Norwich to ask about joining the service and was hoping to go to a radio training school. I asked her if her father had given her the package I had left. She smiled and nodded, saying, "Thank you so much for what you've done." Somehow I don't think that she realized it was stolen property. When I told her what had happened, she informed me, "That wasn't my father but my uncle who was so gruff to you."

When I found this bit of news, I said to myself, "Thank God it wasn't her pop." I asked about her parents, because I figured not very many people could have lived in the farmhouse together. She looked down and whispered that they had been killed in London in 1940 during the Blitz. It wasn't either the first or last time that I said to myself, "If you think you've got it tough, Picardo, just look around." Damn it, I wanted this bloody war to be over. It had brought so much sadness down on so many peoples' lives.

A few days later, Helen left for the service. I wished her well. Like so many times before and after that during the war, it would be the last time I would ever see someone who had been a significant person in my life, if even for only a short while. Helen disappeared from sight. The Red Cross van doughnuts were never the same without her.

Women on Base

Behind our squadron quarters on the base was a vacant lot. In the summertime, English girls would put up pup tents that slept two. And these tents were open for business, if you know what I mean. The authorities didn't seem to care about their presence on base in the middle of a war. I suppose they thought they were good for GI morale or something. Who knows? No one ever really talked about it. They were a wartime reality, and that was all.

Personally, I never fooled with them. Not that I didn't want to, but I was too afraid of VD. But some of the other guys did. Every now and then, we would get these girls some food from the mess hall. Whenever we lost a crew, we would have empty bunks in our hut. One morning when we did have some empty bunks, a girl with long red hair let herself into the hut. She asked me if she could sleep in one of the empty bunks. I told her, "Take any one you want." In no time, she was sound asleep. Business must have been good that night, and she was looking to find forty undisturbed winks. Funny that to do this she needed to come into a hut with a bunch of GIs!

About an hour after she arrived, someone came into the hut and informed us that the captain was on his way to inspect the place. This only happened about every three weeks. Fortunately, they were never very tough on us, because in three weeks we could lose more than a few crews and some of the guys just wouldn't be around anymore. In that kind of environment they took it easy on us.

In response to the captain's imminent arrival, I grabbed an overcoat and threw it over the sleeping woman's head and back, doing my best to cover up her lovely red hair. The captain walked in and someone yelled, "Attention!"

The captain responded with the standard, "At ease." He walked around and, within a matter of seconds, pointed at the bunk where the girl was sleeping peacefully.

I said, "He was on guard duty last night, sir."

He nodded and looked around some more, spotting an empty bottle of scotch on the floor. He said, "I'll be back in about a month. Do you think you can get rid of that empty bottle by then?"

We answered in unison, "Yes sir!" Without further ado, he walked out. I always wondered afterwards what the captain would have done, had he pulled the overcoat off our guest. I'm glad I never found out.

CHAPTER THREE

Rest and Recreation in an English Castle

After our crew had flown seventeen bombing missions, the enlisted men were sent off for seven days of R & R at a small castle near King's Lynn. The officers were sent to a resort in Southampton.

Ours was a beautiful castle, with enormous dining and living rooms. What fascinated me most, though, were the huge bathrooms in multi-colored tile. The bedrooms were large too, with four or five beds in each room. There was about an acre of lawn reaching down to a small river.

Counting the other crews, there were about twenty-five of us altogether. The first thing the organizers did was give us civilian clothes. I loved it—it was wonderful to be out of drab brown for once. I received a pair of blue pants, and red, white and blue shirts. Very patriotic. The first day we arrived, we had five o'clock cocktails prior to dinner. I had never been to a cocktail party in my life. Later we were served dinner in the dining room. Local volunteers and Red Cross workers served us.

After dinner every evening, local girls were bussed in. These girls were always very polite. Some were shy. We would dance to records, and there was always punch and some kind of snack. Tea was omnipresent, but booze was nonexistent. Sometimes the girls would arrive, and we would all watch a movie. These were mostly American films, which were our favorites. Of course, I would tell any English girl willing to listen that I was from North Hollywood. I would make up stories about the place, but I had to stay away from other members of my crew because they would start laughing and blow the whole thing.

If we didn't dance or watch a movie at the castle, we would pile into army trucks and they would drive us into town for a dance or maybe visit a pub or cinema. During this week, the war seemed so far away. There were no air raid sirens, no enemy bombers, no V-2 rockets, not even the sputter of a buzz bomb. It was like heaven.

In the afternoons we would spend our time playing baseball or soccer against other R & R military homes, making bets with the other teams. I can remember vividly the first day of walking into the castle. I saw a bunch of cups and trophies sitting over the fireplace that the former military residents of this castle had won prior to our arrival. By the time we left, the fireplace was bare. We had lost every cup. We also went horseback riding. Well, sort of. I somehow got a horse that must have been very smart. All he wanted to do once I mounted him was go back to the barn. He probably realized there was no future for him in lugging this guy around.

After seven days of total relaxation it was heartbreaking to have to leave. I had had fun, meeting a lot of terrific people I would never see again. Of course, that's common in wartime, but what was difficult about this is that it didn't seem like a war at all. Giving back those civilian clothes was hard to do. We said our good-byes and headed for the train station. Once there, reality started to sink in. There was a war on, and I figured we would have to fly at least thirteen more bombing missions to be through with it. If there were enough crews around, maybe we would finish at thirty. As it turned out, I had only just flown over half of my required missions, but I didn't know it at the time. Would I still be as lucky as I had been up to this point? After all, the Germans weren't firing ping pong balls at us.

While heading for our base on the train, one of the guys said, "I'm going to miss that tile bathroom."

Another said, "To heck with the bathroom, I'm going to miss those five o'clock cocktails." For me, it was the civilian clothes. We had had our morsel of civilian life, now it was back to the bitter taste of war. If I had it all to do over again, I would have settled for a three-day pass. It would have been easier psychologically. But after flying my eighteenth and nineteenth missions, I found myself completely back to reality again and feeling fine.

Spencer always used to tell me that I was the eyes in the back of his head. "Stay awake back there," he would say. One of the responsibilities of the tail gunner was to be a kind of cameraman. Before take off I would set up a camera in the tail section about three or four feet behind the tail turret. The camera was focused through a small hole about the size of a nickel. When we released our bombs, the camera would take pictures of our bomb drop, in order to see how accurate the group's strike was. There were about four or five cameras in the group. Immediately after a mission, the film from these cameras would be developed and analyzed closely by Intelligence. From this film, intelligence would decide if more bombing missions were necessary against the target in question.

Worse than hearing the generic "oil refinery," though, was "oil refineries at Hamburg." For some reason, the Hamburg refineries seemed to be the most heavily defended targets. And when those words were uttered we all stared at each other and someone would whisper in an audible voice, "Oh shit!"

Starting a bombing mission on Hamburg seemed just like going after any other target. But a few hours later you knew you were over Hamburg because the flak was so intense. While on the bomb run, the Germans would track us with flak, but when we finally arrived over the target, they sent up a huge barrage. The worst thing we could hear in a cloud of flak is a noise like the slamming of doors. When we heard that, we could be sure that the shrapnel was penetrating our aircraft. All we could do at that point was bear down, pray, and hope the flak wasn't penetrating the engine casings. That would be bad news indeed.

One morning we learned that a group of B-17s had visited Hamburg the day before, but they had missed the target. The briefers informed us ominously, "The Krauts will be expecting you today."

CHAPTER THREE

At that point I piped up, "If they're expecting us today, why don't we fool them and go tomorrow?" As you can imagine, my suggestion wasn't appreciated by the strategists. We would be in the air over Hamburg just a few hours later. It was to be our twenty-second bombing mission and our fourth visit to Hamburg. Geez!

About three weeks before this mission we hit the refineries at Hamburg for the third time. Flying northeast over the North Sea, we were experiencing heavy clouds beneath us and light clouds above us. I was hoping the two wouldn't meet, they might abort the mission because of poor visibility. Flying over the northern tip of Holland and heading east, we broke out of the clouds and headed for Hamburg.

We dropped our bombs over the target in a barrage of flack and we quickly banked the St. Christopher to the left, leveled off and headed west. Scofield, our waist gunner, informed us that our left rudder was badly damaged when suddenly our squadron was being attacked by eight Messerschmidt 109s coming in at 5:00 and 7:00 o'clock high.

Everyone of us gunners who could see them opened fire. I could see a stream of tracers filling the skies. *What a sight!* I saw what I believed to be a piece of a wing flying off one of the enemy fighters from my tracers as they screached past us. In a second, they turned sharply and headed east. This time, I saw only seven 109s. One could have gone down.

I thought maybe they were turning back to look for stragglers. Then I spotted, at 7:00 o'clock high, nine

P-51 mustangs screaming through the sky going after them. The chase was on. The Mustangs opened fire but we had distanced ourselves from them and I couldn't see clearly what was happening.

The next day we had heard that thirty-one enemy aircraft were destroyed in the area. We could have never survived without our "little friends."

On our fourth trip the flak was incredibly intense, so much so that when we pulled out of the target area, our oxygen and hydraulic fluid system were shot out, and one of our bulkheads was split. Before that day I had no idea that a B-24 could fly with a split bulkhead, but we stayed in the air somehow. I was also unaware that a plane could fly with two hundred and forty flak holes, which is how many we later counted. Usually when we headed back from a mission, the plane felt much lighter and faster because we had gotten rid of our bombs and about half of our fuel. But that day, our B-24 was sluggish and unresponsive. I knew we were in trouble. This was the third time our hydraulic system was shot out and I was getting tired of it.

Over the intercom I heard the pilot say to the navigator, "Chart a course for Sweden." That's right, Sweden. Although the Germans had occupied Norway, Sweden remained isolated from combat, and its government offered safe haven for the crews of crippled Allied planes. The Swedes would keep airmen there for six months or so and then fly them back to England. But planes only went to Sweden if they were in a lot of trouble or if there were badly wounded airmen aboard. I would say two hundred and fourty flak holes counted a long way toward being in trouble! All the time I tried to think of Sweden rather than our split bulkhead. I kept saying to myself, "Tall blondes, tall blondes." I was willing to let them make me a prisoner of war, that's for sure.

Meanwhile, because of our condition we had dropped down to an elevation of between ten and twelve thousand feet, and some P-51 escorts had dropped down to protect us from any German fighters we might meet on the way. The P-51 outperformed every German prop fighter plane that ever went into the sky. Over fifteen thousand P-51s were built during the War, and it was the best bomber escort fighter by a long shot, because it had the range to take us over a German or French target and back again. From what I understand, during the course of World War II, P-51s destroyed over two thousand Axis planes on the ground and over four thousand in the air. The P-38s and P-47s were also good escorts, but they didn't have the range of the P-51s.

I was keeping a keen eye out for what direction we were going and noticed that we kept flying southwest. Dammit! I pointed down in the opposite direction, "Sweden's that way, for Christ's sake." But it became obvious after a while that we weren't going to have a Scandinavian war holiday after all. The crew was absolutely silent, and I would be willing to bet you that my buddies were all thinking the same thing, "Six months vacation from German oil refineries."

It's strange to think of snowbound Sweden as a kind of oasis, but that's the image it conjured up in my head for those few minutes. Looking back on how difficult it was to return to the war after our holiday in England, I think it was probably for the best that we never ended up in Sweden. I can't speak for the rest of the crew, but six months of tall blondes and no flak would have ruined me for combat. To go back into the skies over Germany and France again and again required consistency as much as courage. After a while we got into a rhythm that made the missions and morning briefings bearable. But six months in Sweden? Heck, seven days on a country estate in England was tough enough to come back from as it was.

In the midst of my daydreams over Sweden, I heard the navigator call the pilot, "In two minutes we'll be over the North Sea." Edgar replied, "I hope this thing stays together." My heart fell into my stomach. No way did I want to be in a plane that might crack up over the North Sea, especially considering what we had seen happen to that other B-24 when it went down in the North Sea on that same mission.

From our bomber I could see the crippled B-24 heading toward the sea on the way to an emergency landing. When it hit the water the plane totally broke up. Looking down I could see only two survivors climbing into a raft. I never knew what happened to them but I figured they would have a pretty good chance of making it because they had both the British and American

Navies looking for them. Their buddies probably ended up on the bottom of the sea, though.

Now, don't get me wrong. The B-24 was a great bomber, one of the best ever made, but I didn't want to crack up in one. According to war statistics, the B-24 was the absolute worst plane to ditch in, because it had a survival rating of only twenty-six percent. And you better believe that those odds deteriorated even more when you made an emergency landing on the North Sea, one of the choppiest, stormiest bodies of water you can imagine.

So when Edgar verbalized his doubts about our ability to make it to England I figured our chances were pretty good to end up visiting Davy Jones' locker. A little while later, though, we saw the coast of England. I had never been so happy to see anything in my life. What a view! Better even than a Swedish blonde. Half an hour or so later with a strong head wind, we landed safely at our airfield. All four engines were still running—somehow we hadn't lost a single one. It was the closest thing to a miracle I've ever experienced.

The next day Edgar went to see the line officer in charge of planes shot up during a mission. Now you have to understand that Edgar loved our plane, and he was superstitious about flying in another one. He didn't turn his St. Christopher medal around before every mission for nothing. He believed in luck with the absolute faith of a child. So Edgar, being Edgar, inquired when we could expect to get our plane back. The line officer stared at him in disbelief. "No way you're ever going to see that heap again." He then proceeded to give Edgar a tour of our Liberator and its two hundred and forty flak holes. Whole sections of metal had simply been blown away. Plans were to transform this B-24, Edgar's precious B-24, into scrap iron. You can better believe I wanted a new one. I figured we had used up any amount of good fortune still left in that plane. I was no sentimentalist.

But Edgar was stubborn as a mule, and he understood how to get things done. He didn't waste his time talking to subordinates. No sir, Edgar went right to the seat of power. He made a beeline to Colonel Snavley's office, informed the Colonel of what the line officer had told him, and without batting an eye said simply, "I want my airplane back." Like everyone, the colonel respected Edgar a great deal. He told Edgar to jump into his car with him. They drove back out to the airfield. The colonel walked right up to the offending line officer and pointed back at Edgar, "This man wants his airplane back."

The line officer protested, repeating what he had said to Edgar, but this time you'd better believe he said it in softer tones. He was, after all, speaking to a colonel.

The colonel shook his head at the line officer's objections. "See that he gets his airplane back. That's an order!" Ten days later Edgar and the rest of us got his airplane back. I might have still preferred a new plane, but I had to admit that it was good to sit in my old tail gunner turret. It wouldn't have been the same in another plane. An airman's plane was as much a part of him as his own crew was.

CHAPTER THREE

About three days after we returned from Hamburg, we were given another bombing mission, but had to make do without our own B-24. We were assigned to an older plane on standby. The crew chief of the plane we were flying was probably in his mid-thirties and I referred to him as "the older guy." In the dispersal area where his plane was parked he had built a small hut so that he could stay near his B-24. He loved that plane so much, it was almost like he was married to her. But I guess he wasn't completely faithful because the hut also allowed him to invite his girlfriend to stay out there with him sometimes. When we found out about his regular rendezvous with her we weren't jealous but rather admired his ingenuity. We only wished that we were as clever. Of the crew chief's two loves, though, we were taking away on a mission what I suspect was his more cherished one, and he looked on protectively as we taxied down the runway in preparation for flight.

The bombing mission was, for a bombing mission, pretty uneventful. The target was an aircraft factory at Frankfurt. There were no real problems except for some moderate flak that seemed like nothing when compared to bombing an oil refinery. Hell, you could see the sky the whole time. When we returned to the dispersal area, the crew chief was standing there with both hands on his hips like a jealous lover. He was staring at the left side of the fuselage and the left wing. There were about twenty-five flak holes all together—a far cry from the two hundred and forty we had received the last time out. What did he expect? We hadn't gone out on a joyride! But he was mad as hell, anyway, "Look what you sons of bitches did to my airplane!"

At this point I just had to say, "Gee, we're sorry."

Another crew member responded with less sarcasm that I had, "We didn't do it; the Germans did! At least we brought her back in one piece—we figured you would be glad to see us."

As we walked off to leave the crew chief alone with his plane, Edgar whispered under his breath, "That's one airplane you can be sure will be topnotch when you get into it." If Edgar had to fly in another plane, he wanted to fly in a plane someone loved as much as he loved ours.

You would be right to say that we were petrified as hell of bombing oil refineries. But it's safe to say that the oil refineries were even more frightened of Allied bombers, especially the B-17s and B-24s.

The B-24 had twice the bomb bay capacity than the B-17 and flew farther and faster. All of the B-24s were stationed in the northeast of England known as Norfolk. The B-17s were stationed in the southeast about 100 miles closer to the targets in Europe. When both types of planes were used to bomb a particular target, the B-17s had to take off an hour earlier and land an hour later than the B-24s. The B-17s could and did fly higher though, to avoid the flack. The B-17 defended itself with twelve .50-caliber machine guns. The B-24 only had eight.

During bombing operations in World War II, the 2nd Bomb Division of the 8th Air Force lost 1,458 B-24

Liberators, and 6,032 airmen were killed. We flew a total of 95,948 sorties on 493 operational missions. The Division was awarded six presidential citations and five individuals received the Medal of Honor, the highest award given by the military. With heavy fighter opposition on many occasions on the way to their assigned targets, the 44th Bomb Group claimed over three-hundred and twenty five enemy aircraft destroyed.

At one briefing the officers remarked that the 8th Air Force had knocked out four-fifths of German oil during the war. I never understood why they didn't say eighty percent—it sounded so much better. I leaned over to the crewman next to me, "Well, let's go after the other fifth." This was the American winner-take-all attitude of World War II. We weren't going to settle for anything but unconditional surrender, and we weren't going to be satisfied with anything short of the absolute destruction of the Axis war machine.

Some Tragic Bombing Missions

One of the crews in our hut had a radio operator named Bill Stern. He told us he was the nephew of Bill Stern, the sports announcer who had a radio show on Friday nights and broadcast the Notre Dame games. It was easy to believe, because he looked and talked like him. His ambition was to be a stand-up comedian, so he would try out his routines on us. They were pretty funny the first couple of times. I kept telling him to get new routines.

As I told you, when I was stationed in Massachusetts, we were told that when we got to England, all we would have was a bed mat and a coarse wool blanket, so I stole a sheet and took it with me to England. As far as I know, I was the only one in the 44th Bomb Group with a sheet. Everybody wanted to know where I got it, and they all wanted it. I was offered big bucks for that sheet, but I never gave it up. There was one fellow who waited to see if I came back every time from a bombing mission, so he could be the first in line to grab that sheet. Whenever there was a windy day I would wash it, because when I put it on the clothes line in the wind, it would dry faster. And I had to guard it until it would dry. Bill Stern had a pair of civilian boots that I admired very much. We made an agreement that if he went down, I got the boots. If I went down, he got the sheet.

One day we were both flying on the same mission. After we dressed, the trucks came to take us to the mess hall for breakfast. Bill and I were running late, and we missed the trucks. We were only a couple blocks away, so we walked to the mess hall. While we were walking, a black cat appeared. Bill wouldn't let that cat cross his path. He said, "Come on. Let's walk around it." He wanted me to go with him into a large field to get around that cat.

"You're crazy," I told him. "I'm going to get my breakfast."

I was just finishing breakfast, when he came in huffing and puffing. "I got around that cat," he said, "so I'm going to be all right today." He must have figured my chances of surviving were not very good. The target that day was the marshalling yards at Koblenz.

Coming back out of Germany towards Belgium, we ran into what they call "soup," a bank of thick clouds that obscured just about everything. We had been flying in such tight formation that I could read the small lettering on the plane next to me. When we went into the soup, the order was given to disperse. We were descending rapidly, and there were planes so close to us I thought any moment we would collide with one. I was so scared I couldn't cry or pray. Fortunately about ten minutes later (the longest ten minutes of my life), when we came out of the soup around five thousand feet, the navigator said, "We're over Dunkirk," and the nose gunner shouted, "I can see England." What a relief.

The crew that Bill Stern was on did not get back. A colonel was flying with Bill's crew that day, and the last they heard was the colonel yelling at the pilot to believe his bank-and-turn instrument. Evidently, the pilot felt differently than what his instrument was telling him. He tried to straighten out the plane according to how he felt, and the plane went into a spin and crashed. A few days later they found an oxygen bottle washed ashore, with the serial number of Bill's plane stamped on it. They must have gone down over the English Channel. I couldn't touch those boots....

When Bill Stern and his crew went down, it meant a new crew would soon be moving into our hut. When they arrived a couple of days later, we sized each other up as crews always did, finding out a little about each one. Sooner or later, they would ask, "What's it like flying a bombing mission?"

I would always tell them, "If you can see your fighter escorts, your chances are damn good."

Someone was once asked what it was like to fly bombing missions. I think he hit the nail on the head when he said, "Hours of boredom and moments of sheer terror." Fear is something that you have to keep under control. It can be contagious, so you don't talk about it much. It's something you don't spread around. I believe that my crew did an excellent job of keeping it under control.

The pilot of the new crew was named Shelan. There was a waist gunner on the crew, an Italian from Boston, named Tony. He was tall and, I guess you would have to say, damn good-looking, but quiet and very nervous. Nothing like me. I was short and always loud and obnoxious. I thought that his nervousness was because he was going to fly bombing missions over Germany and France. One day I was talking to the radio operator of the crew, Nick, a big ugly guy whose father worked in the steel mills in Pittsburgh. Nick figured when the war was over, he would follow in his father's footsteps and go to work in the steel mills.

Nick didn't like Tony much. He said, "That damn guy, all he likes to do is look at himself in the mirror." If I looked like Tony, I thought, I would have looked at myself in the mirror, too. Maybe Nick was jealous of Tony's

good looks. Nick told us the reason Tony acted the way
he did. When they left the states for England, Tony had
written letters to his wife and his girlfriend, telling them
how much he was going to miss them and how he couldn't
wait to be in their arms again. He felt that he had goofed
big time, because he believed he had put his girlfriend's
letter into his wife's envelope, and vice versa, and then
mailed them. That's why he was so nervous. Tony would
walk around the hut mumbling, waiting for his mail.

Well, about two weeks later, after flying a couple
of bombing missions during which he did well, he finally
heard from his wife. The unthinkable had happened. His
wife, who was Italian, did get the girlfriend's letter. None
of us, especially Nick, could keep from laughing, but Tony
was very upset. I guess flying bombing missions was a
piece of cake compared to what he had to face when he
got home.

One morning at briefing, we learned the target
that day was the submarine pens at Saint Nazaire,
France. Shelan's crew was supposed to fly off our right
wing. When we hit our target, the flak was moderate to
heavy, but not too accurate because of some cloud cover-
age over the area. Heading for England, Shelan's bomber
ran into trouble. All four of their propellers went out
of control. The way I understand it, an out-of-control
propeller could possibly pull your wing right off the
aircraft, so it's best to just bail out. I watched and
counted all nine chutes opening. With the high regard
we had for the French Underground, we figured there was

a good chance they would be picked up and in time, get back to England.

But if I were in Tony's shoes, I might have just stayed in France; or, if his wife had a large family with a father, brothers and uncles, I think I would have just headed for Italy and moved in with relatives. Three months later when I left England, we still had not heard a thing from Shelan's crew. It had only been the crew's sixth bombing mission.

One morning they told us our target was an oil refinery at Brunswick. On these missions we were always told how much flak we would encounter and where the enemy fighter fields were located in the area of the target. They would always say, "We do expect some losses." There was a navigator by the name of Kurt who was a very close friend of our navigator. I never really knew if they were from the same town or met in the service at navigation school, but they were close friends. That morning, the navigator of a crew that was scheduled to fly had the flu. Kurt, who was not scheduled to fly that day, volunteered to fly so the crew could go. We all had dispersal areas where the planes were parked. The plane he was flying in was parked next to ours. I can remember our navigator over there talking to Kurt before take-off.

In the nose of the B-24 were "blisters," a bubble you can stick your head up into, to see the ground or more of the sky. On the bomb run that day, as he was looking out of the blister, a shell exploded, the suction tearing off the blister and also Kurt's head. When we landed and looked over at the plane that Kurt had been flying in, we could see his body lying on a cot, covered completely except for his boots. Our navigator looked over there with a very hurt look. None of us knew what to say. We just stood there waiting for the trucks to come and take us to the de-briefing room. After the de-briefing, I never saw our navigator again. The next day the pilot came and told us that he had been grounded and reassigned. I was madder than hell and I said, "At least you could have given us a chance to say good-bye."

All the pilot said was, "You couldn't have." Our navigator had become disoriented and upset.

One of my saddest memories occurred during a mission to bomb the railway center at Saarbrucken. This was a large depot supplying ammuniton to the Western Front. During bombing our P-51 escort would use auxiliary fuel tanks. These tanks were attached under the fuselage and released when enemy aircraft were sighted.

My adrenaline always surged at the sight of these falling tanks for it meant the fight had begun.

But at Saarbrucken, for reasons never explained to us, before or after, our P-51s were fitted with auxiliary tanks under each wing instead of under the fuselage. S2 should have informed us of this change at the morning briefing. This turned out to be a tragic decision. You see, when fitted with wing tanks, the P-51 Mustang bears a strong resemblance to the German ME 210, a twin-engine fighter which some bomber groups did encounter.

It was on our way to the IP that I first noticed two of our fighters approach our formation. This wasn't unusual if they were ours. What was odd was the appearance of objects under the wings.

I had been trained at Harlingen, Texas, to quickly ID various aircraft, both enemy and friendly, but this was unusual.

Two fighters, potentially deadly to our bomb-laden Liberators, approaching slowly but resembling an ME 210. It's hard to explain why you act a certain way in a situation that requires an instant decision, but these planes weren't slashing at our formation in an attacking way and their tail rudders were squared like the P-51s and not oval like the ME 210s. I held my fire. Gunners on other bombers did not, and sent a stream of .50-caliber bullets at the planes. Their aim was true and the fuel tank on one of the Mustangs was hit and exploded, engulfing the plane in flames, and then it too exploded. The pilot had no chance. I heard later the other fighter was also destroyed but I didn't see it.

We bombed the target successfully, leaving the railway center in flames, but my thoughts on that mission always go back to that fighter and his unfortunate death. I also reflect on what Marco, my sergeant back in basic training said about learning all that you possibly can before going into combat, *"It may save you and your buddies."*

On subsequent missions I noticed our fighter escorts kept a good deal further away from us.

I didn't blame them.

CHAPTER THREE

One morning our target was an aircraft field and factory at Stuttgart. On the way there, we flew past Frankfurt but out of the way of any flak. Over Stuttgart the flak was moderate to heavy, and we left there with some minor damage. On our way home, we were supposed to pass near Frankfurt but out of the range of any flak. The formation was two degrees off course. That put us in the range of the flak guns over Frankfurt. They opened up with a barrage. We had thought we were home free, but we were in the range of their guns. The next thing I heard Stewart say was, "George has been hit." My stomach felt sick. He was hit in the face and neck. The blood coming from his cheek had hidden the wounds in his neck, so we thought he was only hit in the cheek. It was so cold with the waist windows open that his blood froze on his skin, and the bleeding stopped. Spencer asked Stewart, "Do you need any help?" Stewart answered, "No, I can handle it." They used to have little tubes of morphine that we would stick in the veins to kill the pain. But George said he had no pain.

About an hour later he started to feel pain, so Stewart gave him some morphine. As we got closer to home and decreased our altitude, the bleeding started again. When you have wounded aboard and you shoot a yellow flare, they let you come right in and land. We shot our flare, landed, and an ambulance was right there to take George away. I remember the smell of blood nauseated me. The next day we went to see George in the hospital. "How are they treating you?" we asked.

"Pretty good," he said. "Once I found out how to get some attention. Yesterday I was lined up in the hall with all the wounded on stretchers. I was hurting, so I said, 'Oh, Jesus Christ!' The doctor pointed to me and said, 'He's next!' "

George could have gone home, but we had about ten missions to fly. He stayed there and welcomed us back from every bombing mission. Our crew was like that.

Once, on our way back from a bombing mission, we were hit by flack while leaving the enemy's coast. The flack penetrated our plane, a small piece hitting just below Tom Stewart's right ankle. After we landed and finally got back to our hut, he pulled the shrapnel out with his fingers. He managed to stop the bleeding and bandaged it himself.

Spencer found out about it and came charging into our hut. "Tom," he said, "You get to the medics right away!" Tom begged, "Don't make me go, they will ground me! I want to keep flying with my crew!" Finally Spencer gave in, "Okay, but we will keep a close eye on it for any infection."

Stewart's injury healed fine. What a guy!

A good-natured kid named Abercrombie, from Atlanta, Georgia, stepped in for George. We were happy to have him.

Angela

I didn't know that my fourth visit to London was going to be my last. While walking down Picadilly, one of the main business streets in London, I spotted a tailor shop. I needed to have some tailoring done, so I stopped in. When I walked in, a bell rang. I was in a comfortable waiting room with a sofa, chairs and a lamp next to one of the chairs. An elderly man walked in and asked me what he could do for me. I showed him my sergeant stripes and told him I wanted them sewn on to my new flight jacket. He said, "Come with me." We walked through a room where a gentleman was being fitted for a new sport jacket.

The elderly man pointed to a small room and said, "Go in there, Yank. There's a young lady who can help you." I took one look at her and right away I was aroused. She was a doll, petite with a slim waist, olive-colored skin, black hair, and beautiful features. I showed her what I wanted done. She smiled and said, "That won't take long."

I told her I was from North Hollywood. She wasn't impressed. She said her name was Angela, and she was from Portugal. She spoke perfect English with no accent. It was hard for me to believe that she was from Portugal. I was very much attracted to her. I lied and told her it was my first time in London and I hadn't seen any of the sights and really didn't know my way around. She said, "Everyone should visit London at least once." I kept talking, trying to impress her. Finally, when she finished sewing, she picked up the conversation, wondering what it was like flying in a plane and being shot at.

Finally I just came out and asked her, "What do you like to do?" Without blinking an eye she said, "I like to f—," and used the four-letter word. I was shocked; my knees actually buckled. That was one word we didn't use much in those days. I know I didn't. I said to myself, "This girl is not from Portugal." It was early in the afternoon and I told her I was free for the evening and I would like to take her out when she was off work.

Angela agreed, on conditions which included: first dinner, then a show, and I had to pay her one English pound if we went to bed. I figured what better way to get your mind off the war. One English pound was about four American dollars at that time.

To hell with the VD film, I had my condoms. I was to pick her up later when she got off work. I was staying with the guys at a hotel nearby. I tried to get a room at the same hotel, but none was available. I got myself a cab and told the driver to find me a hotel room. He said, "I'll take you to Russell Square. There are always some available there." We found a nice hotel and I got a small room on the second floor. I was all set.

Later I picked her up. She was standing by the shop and looked like she had put on fresh make-up. I told her she looked great. Make-up was hard to come by during the war. She wanted to go to a restaurant called "The American." She said they had good food there. The name "American" was a come-on, though. Dinner was the usual piece of meat with boiled Brussels sprouts, potato and unsweetened desserts. But they did serve Scotch.

From there, she wanted to go to a service club where Vera Lynn was appearing. She was Angela's favorite. Vera put on a two-hour variety show with singers, dancers and a comedian. Angela seemed to enjoy it very much.

CHAPTER THREE

Leaving the club it was foggy, and with the blackout we couldn't see much of the city. We got ourselves a cab and headed for Russell Square. When reaching the hotel I was hoping she wouldn't mind the smallness of our room. The air-raid siren started sounding, which wasn't unusual in London. I don't think she noticed the room. We started playing around and ended up in bed.

When going for our second climax, I heard that sputtering sound that I heard so many times at the base. It was the V-1 Buzz Bomb. All I could think was, "Oh no, not tonight!" Looking up, I heard the sputtering stop. That meant it had run out of gas and was falling. My thing, like a rocket hurrying to be launched from its pad, melted like a candle. Then there was a big explosion, the building shaking, plaster falling down from the walls of our room, plaster dust all over the place. Angela was screaming, I jumped up, put my pants on and opened our door.

Running down the hall, I saw a couple trying to cover their private parts with their clothes. The woman was crying, and the guy was white as a sheet. I shut the door. Angela and I dressed. She was shaking like a leaf, wanting to get out of there and away from the building. Once outside, fire trucks and aid cars showed up. Angela held on to me, and we started walking. We must have walked about ten blocks before we were able to get a cab. When we got in the cab, she wanted to go to her flat.

We drove across town to her place. She jumped out and barely waved good-bye. How could I blame her?

I think you've almost got to lose your life to know how to live it. The cab driver said to me, "She's in bad shape, but she'll get over it. We always do. During the London Blitz, I took some of the wounded to the hospital in my cab and even some dead to the morgues." I said to myself, "This guy has seen a lot."

When I got back to my hotel, the guys were up, nursing a bottle of Scotch. They asked, "Where have you been? How did your clothes get so dirty?" They heard there were a few buzz bombs dropping in the area.

"Those Germans," one said, "they always send them over when it is foggy, so the Spitfires can't see them." I told them what had happened. Wide-eyed, they all listened. When I finished they all started laughing.

One said, "I bet at least seven guardian angels have quit trying to protect you!" I told them, "No more passes to London!" If the enemy was going to get me, I wanted it to be after we dropped our bomb load.

All of a sudden, it dawned on me, "My God, I forgot to give her that one English pound." I guess I will always owe her those four bucks.

Shell Lodged In Number Three Engine

One morning in the fall of 1944, we were scheduled for another bombing mission. I was getting up early with the guys when I heard someone say, "I hope we'll be lucky again today." Comments like this were common to hear in the mornings.

CHAPTER THREE

Hurrying to the briefing after a good breakfast of French toast, bacon and hot coffee, we were informed that the target for the day was a large aircraft engine factory at Bremen, a large city in northwest Germany. If we hit that factory, we knew it would never produce engines for fighters that might knock us out of the skies for good.

Whenever we flew over the North Sea or the English Channel, we would be escorted to the enemy coast by British Spitfires, at which point our P-51 Mustangs picked up escort duty. We knew the Spitfires were reliable, but I always loved the sight of those Mustangs. On our way to Bremen we knew that we would be flying over at least three enemy fighter airfields, so we kept our eyes wide open. Sure enough, just before we started our bomb run we heard the fateful sentence, "Bandits in the area!"

We hit our IP, turned and started our bomb run and headed for the target. Fishbone left his radio and turned the switch that opened the bomb bay doors. At that moment, the flak started coming up. Following bomber logic, we felt a little safer, knowing that the German fighters would be unlikely to pursue us in the midst of all the flak. As we approached the target, the flak got heavier and heavier. All we could do was fly as quickly through as possible, drop our payload and hope for the best. We dropped our bombs, banked to the right and got out of the cloud of flak. Edgar directed the B-24 toward our fighter escorts.

As the tail gunner, I probably had the best view of the target. I recognized the factory complex from the aerial photo shown to us at the briefing. It was completely covered with smoke—it looked like a great hit to me.

The bomber was still banking to the right to get away from all the flak, when out of nowhere appeared four German ME-109 fighters. The nose gunner informed us they were headed toward us at about eleven o'clock and he started firing. Firing their nose cannons at us, they dove through the formation at a terrific speed, crossing over me at about four o'clock. I started firing, following my tracers. A moment later, I saw our fighters head out after them. With our Mustangs in pursuit of the Germans, we felt a lot safer. Or so we thought.

The copilot, Frank Collela, made an announcement over the radio. "Hey you guys, there's a shell lodged in between two cylinder heads of our number three engine." Frank had a view of the disturbing sight, because the number three engine was just outside his window, a few feet away. No member of our crew said a word. It was probably the only time during the entire war that our crew was completely silent. I said to myself, "How is it possible for that shell to be lodged between our cylinder heads when it had to pass between three fast-rotating propellers to get there?"

Frank tried to rouse us again. "There's a shell lodged in our number three engine. It looks like a twenty-three millimeter." Again, silence.

Finally, I couldn't stand it anymore. Being a smart ass, I said "Do you want me to climb out on the wing and kick it off?" What do you do when you've got a shell lodged in one of your engines, twenty-one thousand feet over Germany? Not a damn thing, that's what. We were all thinking the same thing: Could it really be a dud? All we could do to find out was to sweat it out and hope. If the shell did explode, there was a better than even chance that it would take the wing with it, and we would be headed straight down. We had no choice but to stay in formation, but our wing men sure kept their distance. We were all very concerned, believe me.

Heading for England, we crossed the enemy coast over Holland, still at twenty-one thousand feet. Once we reached the North Sea, we dropped to about ten thousand feet. The air was heavier there, and we were bound to bounce a bit more. This made us a little nervous normally, but with a shell in our number three engine, it was terrifying.

Flying over England, we knew we would be landing in about twenty minutes. We all wanted to be walking on the ground, but we also wanted to avoid jostling that damn shell too much. When our wheels hit the runway, it jarred the plane a bit, but nothing happened. Whew, it felt wonderful to be on the ground again. Once parked in the dispersal area, we all hurried out to take a look at the wayward shell which, by all rights, should have killed us. Even the ground crew and crews from other planes crowded around, amazed.

A pilot who had flown behind us that day told Spencer, "I never took my eye off of your plane. I expected it to blow at any minute."

A few minutes later, the English technical people showed up with their ladders and repair equipment, telling us to clear away from the aircraft. One of the airmen claimed, "The shell has got to be a dud."

Another said, "You're crazy. It can't be."

The point of the shell was about one inch from hitting the wing. Some claimed that had the shell hit the wing, it would certainly have exploded. At this juncture, though, the discussion was academic. We were on the ground, and that was all that mattered. At the debriefing, they informed us that there had been about two hundred and fifty enemy fighters in the area. The P-51s had gotten the better of the Luftwaffe that day. The following day we heard that one of our pilots had shot down five bandits. A helluva good day's work! All we could do was sit and wait for the next mission.

It was on the very next bombing mission in the fall of 1944 that we spotted the first jets the Germans sent up. We were over the Zeider Zee, Holland, coming out of Germany and headed for home, when suddenly we spotted the first ME 262. It went through our formation so fast and turned so sharply that I wondered if it weren't really a runaway missile. It seemed to have double the speed of our fighters. All of a sudden, it turned and headed east.

When we arrived at our base, S2 was informed. We had a massive meeting that night. Intelligence was very concerned about the possibility of a new air war. But as it turned out, those jets weren't all that effective. A lack of fuel seemed to hamper their performance. Bombing those oil refineries really paid off!

CHAPTER THREE

The Battle of the Bulge

In 1944, the Allied armies were fighting their way across France toward the German border. After the success of D-Day, the war seemed all but won, though everyone knew there would be many bloody days before everything was finally settled and Hitler and his cronies were finally put in their place forever. No one should ever have underestimated the resolve of the German Army to protect the Fatherland, though. Just before Christmas, we heard that the Germans had broken through our lines of defense and were headed toward Bastogne.

On December 22, we got up early and readied ourselves for a bombing mission in support of our boys on the ground. Up until that point, we had always flown strategic bombing missions. Those were missions flown into Germany to take out oil refineries, factories, railroad yards and submarine pens. These kinds of missions were designed to take the heat out of the German war machine, directed at long-term consequences. By contrast, what we were going to do at the end of 1944 was to fly a tactical mission with short-term goals. We were going to fly in direct support of the troops. We had never done anything like this before. We would only be up for four or five hours—for strategic missions deep into Germany, we could sometimes be up for twice that length of time.

Our target that day was a railroad junction about thirty miles north of our troops. The Germans were bringing in supplies through this junction. These supplies had to be shut down in order to give our troops a better chance at victory. We went to our aircraft, waiting and waiting for the foggy English weather to clear up. But it didn't. After a couple of hours, the mission was canceled. We were disappointed, because we were anxious to do something to stem the resurgent German tide. We went through the same procedure on December 23 and with the same result. The mission was canceled again.

By now, Bastogne was surrounded. Our troops were desperately short of ammunition and medical supplies. The German artillery was causing most of the damage with its tanks, but our fighters couldn't get to them because of the terrible weather. The elements seemed to be on the side of the Germans in this fight. Hitler needed that kind of weather to keep the Allied bombers and fighters grounded. Once again, on Christmas Eve, we rose early to fly. Finally, the weather did clear, and we took off. It was a great feeling to know that we were going to be able to do something to help. This was to be my thirty-first bombing mission.

The group left England and headed for the enemy coast. Just before reaching it, we lost an engine because of mechanical failure. We feathered the prop, turned around and headed back for England. What a disappointment! We wanted this one so much we could taste it. On December 26, the 44th Bomb Group took off again to hit the German supply lines. We leveled a marshaling yard in western Germany that had been instrumental in getting supplies out to the German troops. It felt good to be a part of this battle. For some reason we weren't concerned about the flak. We wanted this one.

Last Mission

On December 31, 1944, just a week or so after our Battle of the Bulge mission, we flew our last combat mission. Doing it on New Year's Eve somehow made sense. When 1945 arrived, we would be like the baby new year himself, ready to start our lives over again, free from the death cloud that hung over our heads.

We woke up early in the morning, and you could just feel the excitement in the air. While dressing, I kept saying, "This is the one we've been looking for. Let's make it a good one." I knew Pete, the newlywed, wanted to get back to his wife in Milwaukee. He wanted it even more than I did, if that were possible.

Everyone dressed and waited for the trucks to pick us up and take us to the mess hall for breakfast. When we ate eggs in the morning they were usually powdered, but this morning we had fresh ones. I figured this was a good omen. Things had to go well today. As I was going through the mess line the guy serving put five of them on my plate, all sunny side up. Boy, were they good. When I finished those, I still had some bacon left, so I thought I would go up and get another egg. There were seven eggs already cooked on the grill. I was the only guy around and the server put all seven on my plate, "Take them. I want to clean the grill." This was the first and last time

I ever ate a dozen fried eggs for breakfast. I was stuffed but content.

At the briefing I was praying it wouldn't be an oil refinery, and it wasn't. It turned out to be an ammunition factory in eastern Germany. Target: Neuweied. So far, so good.

When we arrived at our plane, everyone inspected it. The crew chief informed us it was ready to go. Ground crews would work around the clock to get an aircraft ready, especially if it had been shot up badly. They had done a good job on ours that day. "This is the one you guys have dreamed about," they said. "Good luck." It all seemed like a dream, somehow. Could this really be our very last mission? Sometimes it would get so foggy on base that you couldn't ride a bicycle without endangering your life. Today was no exception, and we waited in fear of seeing red flares signaling the mission's cancellation. Suddenly we saw the green flares. The mission was on.

We started our engines and were soon taxiing toward the main runway, ready for takeoff. I was in the back, on the intercom with Edgar, watching the four engines. When we ran out of runway, we were already a few feet off the ground and climbing. Our last takeoff. The engines looked good. We were on our way.

We joined our formation heading over the English Channel toward Belgium. We started looking for our fighter support. Arriving at the coast of Belgium, we banked away from the flak coming up at us and headed east. At about twenty-two thousand feet we spotted our fighter support. That was always a good feeling.

CHAPTER THREE

Suddenly, I started belching from all the eggs I had eaten. The gas was building up like crazy in my stomach. Then I started farting. I was wearing a flying suit, a heated suit, a flak jacket and my oxygen mask. All I could smell were those damn farts. I farted all the way to the target. It was awful.

We reached our IP, turned toward the target and opened our bomb bay doors. The bomb run proceeded normally. All of a sudden, right under me at six o'clock low I saw a Messerschmidt 109, one of the best German fighter planes, popping out of a cloud. The German fighter disappeared into another cloud. When there were clouds around, German fighters were known to try and fly parallel to the Allied bomber formation to determine its altitude, speed and course. But with our fighter support, they never hung around for long.

I was determined that if I saw him again, I was going to blow him out of the sky. There was just no way they were going to get us on our last mission. I had seen crews lose it on their last mission, but it wasn't going to happen to us. Luckily for that German pilot (and maybe, realistically, for us), I never saw that fighter again. But I was so intent on getting it that I forgot to call it in on the intercom. That was a mistake. When any one of us saw an enemy fighter, we were supposed to communicate it to the rest of our crew. They could come at us from any angle.

Finally we were over the target. The flak was pretty heavy, but we dropped our bombs with no problem and banked out of the target area and flak. The first thing I wanted to know was if all four engines were running properly. They were. We had been hit by some flak, but it was nothing serious. As we pulled away from the target, I could see it burning. A moment later we spotted our fighter support. What a beautiful sight. Were we home free? It was a great feeling to be in formation and heading home.

On our way home my farting had finally stopped, and my stomach felt lighter and happier. I decided to serenade the crew with one of my better ballads. This time some of them joined in—that's how happy everyone was. And it was then that I discovered that most of the crew couldn't carry a tune.

Someone up front said, "Hey, I can see the English Channel." The excitement started building up. Soon we were over the channel itself, and we could see England. The bombardier was telling anyone willing to listen that he could hardly wait to walk up and down Pitkin Avenue in uniform.

It was a custom that when a bomber crew had flown its last mission, they would buzz our escort fighter airbase. When we were coming in low to buzz the P-51 field, suddenly a P-51 appeared at six o'clock low. As we buzzed, he came between us and the ground, shooting up in front of the cockpit. Edgar shouted, "What the hell was that? Let's get the hell out of here!"

A couple of months before, two bomber crews from our group were flying their last bombing mission. When they reached the channel, they left the group and started fooling around. I guess it must have been the excitement of the last mission that clouded the judgment of the pilots, but somehow they collided, exploded, and all eighteen men were killed. You never forget it when you see something like that.

As we came in to land, I can remember the wheels hitting the ground. I kept saying to myself, "We've made it! We've made it!" I cannot explain the feeling that came over me. I've tried many times to put it in words, but I never seem to be able to do it. So I've stopped trying.

When we landed and parked our plane, there was Colonel Snavley, the commander of the base, waiting to greet us. He congratulated us and handed us each a big Havana cigar. In those days they were sold for five cents each. I tried to smoke mine but started to get sick, so I gave it to Edgar. When the trucks picked us up and brought us to the briefing room, I saw the Red Cross trucks with their coffee and doughnuts. I missed Helen. I would have liked to have had a chat with her and let her see the excitement.

It was going to be our last debriefing, the best debriefing of all. At all of our debriefings there was always a half bottle of rye. We would never touch it, though. A lot of the other crews would ask for it and we were always happy to pass it over to them. Not this time. We all had a shot. Pete made a toast, "Milwaukee, here I come!"

That night we planned to have a big New Year's Eve party. It didn't last long, though. We were so tired that by ten-thirty we were all fast asleep.

A few days later someone asked me, "Eddie you must have been very brave to fly in that tail turret?" "No'" I replied, "I just didn't know any better!"

And that's the truth.

CHAPTER FOUR
Coming Home

Thirty-three bombing missions. There wouldn't be a thirty-fourth. My career as a tail gunner was completed, and somehow I was going to walk away from the war in one piece. I could hardly believe it. It's a good thing I hadn't been able to take out twenty thousand dollars in insurance. If I had, it would have been wasted money. My crew and I were preparing for the return home. The only thing left to do was wait for shipping-out orders.

A waist gunner buddy of mine, named Les, from another crew had a couple more missions to fly. He wanted me to hang around after my crew left and instruct new gunner crews. He said to me, "Look, we can eat at our own mess hall as well as the ground crew's. Hell, we can eat six meals a day." Half a dozen army meals a day was Les' only argument for sticking around.

Les was a six-foot-two strapping blonde Midwesterner. He was a handsome kid. He loved that warm English beer, but every time we would walk into a pub together, beer didn't seem to matter that much, because the girls would just gawk at him. In order for me to get some attention, I had to pull my North Hollywood origins out of the hat. The girls would say, "North Hollywood, how far is that from Hollywood?" I would always tell them, "My dad's café is one block from Hollywood." The English don't measure distances in blocks, so I don't know if they understood how far away that is, but I guess it sounded damn close to the glittering lights of Tinsel Town.

Saying Good-bye to My Crew

Staying with Les in England would be fun, but saying good-bye to my own crew was extremely difficult. I really loved those guys. By the end of the war they were like brothers to me. We decided to have a party, and at this party we ended up playing poker. For some reason that night, I couldn't lose. I had never won like that before. As it all turned out, it was terrible timing. I ended up winning all of their money, but I had to give it all back. I couldn't very well send them home with no money in their wallets.

The next morning I met them at the plane before their departure. We talked and laughed. Pete was so excited about seeing his new bride again. When they said good-bye, a part of me left with them. I felt good about having given them their money back. And although we promised to keep in touch, as time went by, we contacted one another less and less.

In Trouble Again

When Les and I became instructors, we had to show an outdated training film for gunner crews. This film showed gunners how to aim, lead and fire in two-second bursts. Although the film was obsolete, we were required to show it anyway. By this time, of course, the Germans were fighting the air war with cannons in their fighter planes. This changed the calculus of the air war entirely. Rather than shoot their .50-caliber guns at our bombers from afar, the Germans would dive straight through a formation and fire a shell aimed at the bomber's wings where the gas was stored. If the shell hit this part of the wing, the bomber would explode. End of story.

With this strategy, the fighters would come in so fast that we didn't have time to aim, lead the aircraft and then fire. All we could do was follow our tracers. In a single second, the German fighter would have disappeared. Without our fighter support, Allied bombers would have simply disappeared.

There was a pub about half a mile from our base, and because I had a lot more free time, I spent more time off base than ever before. Les and I taught one ninety minute class in the morning and one in the afternoon, and we would get every third day off.

Les and I spent a lot of time at this pub. One night, Les had too many beers. On the bicycle trip home, we would come to a small canal and have to take a left over a tiny bridge. But Les never took a left. He kept going and just fell in the canal. When I heard the splash, I stopped, backtracked and jumped in after him. We were damn lucky the canal was only about five feet deep because I can't swim. I don't know who got who out of the water, but if it had been any deeper, they would still be looking for us. Trying to get someone who has had too much to drink back to the base on a bicycle can be more than a bit of a problem.

On another night, I met a woman at the pub who had a beautiful young daughter. She was about eighteen or nineteen, and she wanted to go to Hollywood and become a big movie star. Normally a girl like that would have been more interested in blonde-haired, blue-eyed Les. Well, you had better believe that she was more interested in a short Italian Yank from North Hollywood. Her mother was sure she would become an instant hit there. Fame and fortune, that's what motivated this mother, not the well-being of her daughter.

The daughter was beautiful, and all she ever did was smile. The mother, a large woman, did all of the talking for herself and her daughter. Every time Les and I would show up, the mother and daughter show would show up about twenty minutes later. Les said to me once, "Someone must let them know when we arrive. That mother must want you to marry her daughter and take her back with you to North Hollywood." I sure as hell had no intention of getting married, but I would have loved to have taken a honeymoon with her somewhere away from her mother.

This mother kept telling me how wonderful her daughter was. It didn't take long for her to become a real pain in the ass. I didn't dare ask the girl out because I figured her mother wouldn't leave us alone. Eventually, though, the mother invited me to her home, but not Les. It was obvious that North Hollywood was on her mind. Les said, "Look, can't you see they're setting you up? They don't give a damn about you. They just want to use you to get to Hollywood!" If an English girl married an American soldier, she would be given first priority to come to the States. But if you planned to bring her over to get married, the paperwork could take months. Les knew about this rule, but I didn't.

Reflecting on my dinner invitation, Les said, "If you end up going, it will cost you. She's going to let you be alone with her daughter, and if you somehow manage to get inside her pants, the mother will run to the colonel and tell him her daughter was a virgin until she met you and that you should do the honorable thing by her. Besides, maybe she's already pregnant with someone else's baby. They don't care about you. If the mother finds out you're really from Seattle, she's big enough to kill you." That did it. Les proved more persuasive about not fraternizing with this English girl than he had about sticking around to instruct gunner crews.

So when I met the English mother-daughter team again, the mother was quick to tell me how disappointed her daughter was that I hadn't come to dinner. I figured that Les had been right about their motives for inviting me to dinner, and it made me mad that I hadn't been able to see it like Les. Burned up, I told the mother that I had missed dinner because of the need for having an operation. I told her I had been circumcised and would have to lay low for a few weeks. She snapped back, "How come you're not walking funny?" I couldn't keep from laughing as I walked away and stayed away.

When Les and I were in England together, it was in the winter time. Coal was rationed and the huts weren't always warm. Les came up with the idea of going to the quartermaster and signing out a truck. "That way," Les said, "we can buy a cord of wood for the hut." If we could solve the heating problem ourselves, the Army would let us do it. So Les and I took off.

We had heard about a small town by the name of Wisbitch and we wanted to know what a town with such a name looked like. So on our way to buy the wood, we headed for Wisbitch. We didn't realize how far away the town was. We arrived there at about twenty minutes after two. The pubs closed from three to five. That didn't give us much time. Wisbitch actually turned out to be a pretty little town, with a river running alongside it. I saw kids getting out of school and walking home. I hadn't seen that in a long time. There were no American soldiers around and no MPs either—just bobbies.

CHAPTER FOUR

We decided to visit the closest pub, even though it closed at three. Les remarked, "I've got forty minutes to drink beer." And Les made the most of his time. He put them down one after another. I couldn't stand the beer, but this pub also had gin. Talking to the lady at the pub, we told her, "We are looking to buy some wood."

"It's a little late to look for wood. I'm closing now," she said, "but I'll open again at five, and there'll be a few girls coming in after work. There's a hotel and restaurant here, too."

Les said he needed to eat some food to settle his stomach. After eating and talking with the local people, we saw that it was already five o'clock. Les suggested we head back to the pub to see what was going on there. We hadn't done a very good job of finding any wood yet.

We enjoyed the girls of Wisbitch a great deal, but by the time we had begun partying with them, it was already dark and we knew we couldn't find our base from there because of the blackout in effect during the war. We knew we were in trouble. We asked the girls if we could spend the night at their place, but they told us that Wisbitch was a small town and everyone knew what went on there. They told us to stay at the hotel, and that's exactly what we did.

We showed up back at the base twelve hours late with no wood and no gas. We were ordered to see Colonel Snavley immediately. When we got there he said, "I'm not going to take your stripes away because you've already flown your tour of duty, but would you two please go home?"

Les and I looked at each other, shrugged and I answered, "Sure, we would be glad to go home."

He nodded, "OK, until your shipping orders come through, you will work with the ground crews." We didn't have a very strong bargaining position with Colonel Snavley.

Bombs Away

When reporting to the ground crew the following night, they assigned us to a jeep with a trailer attached to it. We were to go to the bomb dump, load the trailer with bombs and take it to one of the bombers. The crew there would load them into a bomb bay. A couple of nights later, a chubby little guy was assigned to our work detail. He had been transferred from the infantry to the base because he had flat feet. We took him with us to the bomb dump to load bombs onto the trailer. It was hard work. After loading the trailer, Les got in the driver's seat. I sat next to him in front. I told the guy to sit on top of the bombs. He didn't want to, but I assured him the bombs had no fuses or detonators and could not possibly go off. So we started off, driving to one of the runways, still dark because of the blackout, and headed for one of the bombers.

I made the mistake of saying to Les, "I wonder what this jeep can do, pulling a load." Bang!—the gas pedal went to the floorboard. About two hundred feet later, our right front wheel hit a big chuckhole. We bounced so badly that it nearly threw me out of my seat. The trailer's right wheel also hit the chuckhole, and the trailer bounced just like we had a moment before. The guy and the bombs he was sitting on went rolling off onto the runway. It scared the hell out of me. I thought for sure that he would be crushed to death by those rolling bombs. Les stopped the jeep. Miraculously, the kid stood up, screaming at us. What a relief! He might have chewed us out, but at least he was alive.

The MPs showed up and he told them what happened. "They're crazy!" he said. "I want you to take me back. I won't ride with them!" The MPs made it clear to us that we were to pick up all the bombs, load them and take them to the assigned bomber. It was very hard work, and I was sore for days.

After loading the bombs and delivering them to their assigned bomber, we went back to our huts and fell sound asleep. The next day they informed us that our shipping orders were ready, but there weren't any airplanes heading back to the States at that time. They decided to get us off the base anyway, shipping us off to Southampton and sending us home on the USS *La Juna*, the flagship of our convoy. The convoy consisted of about thirty ships, plus our escorts. One ship was loaded with English war brides. When we discovered that, Les looked at me and laughed. One of those brides probably could have been mine, but she sure would have been disappointed when we ended up in Seattle and not North Hollywood.

As a tail gunner, I was a completely responsible airman, as long as the job had to be done. When the job of flying bombing missions over Germany was over, I immediately went back to my old style of getting into trouble. I guess in all these years, I haven't changed much!

In retrospect, I see that when necessity requires, I focus my total energy on the job to be done. Humor helps me to do this. The Lord has given me the gift of intelligence, the ability to form close, meaningful relationships, and the capacity to see humor in all situations. He has given me the strength to hide my many hurts with humor and laughter, the two most perfect cover-ups. The pain that I felt as a little boy is still with me. But the Lord has provided me with a joy for life that has resulted in a wealth of friends whom I treasure and whose company I enjoy.

I can remember when I finally got home, a millionaire by the name of Louie Navone said to me, "Eddie you've had an experience that with all my money I could never buy. I envy you."

A millionaire envying me. Geez!!!

Heading West

On reaching New York Harbor, we docked at Pier 44. Across from our pier was the *Queen Elizabeth*. It was the biggest ship I had ever seen. It looked like a large hotel. We disembarked from the USS *La Juna*, and on the pier, sure enough, was the Red Cross with coffee and doughnuts, to welcome us back.

We boarded a ferry and zigzagged across New York Harbor to New Jersey. I've never seen so much traffic in such a small harbor. We arrived at a staging area where a band was playing, and people crowded around us to welcome us home.

After about three days of processing, twenty-eight of us were put on a railroad coach, and we headed west toward Fort Lewis, Washington. It felt great passing forests, fields and towns, knowing we were going home. It was spring of 1945, and baseball season was just about to start. Boy, was I looking forward to seeing the old Seattle Indians play again. Only now, they were the Seattle Rainiers, and they played in a new stadium.

Chicago!

One special morning about 9:30 a.m., we came into the Chicago train station. We were moving slowly, and I can remember seeing people waving to us from their tenements and houses. I couldn't understand how they knew that twenty-eight veterans were in one of the cars of a long train. I guess they didn't know, after all. When we arrived at the station, we were told by our leader, Sergeant Wicker, that the Germans had just surrendered. The twenty-eight of us had a four-hour layover in Chicago. We were free to go into town to celebrate, but we had to make sure we were back at the station within four hours.

So four of us took off on our own for downtown Chicago. We walked over a bridge, came to State Street, and—boy! Chicago was going wild. I guess everyone quit work early that day. The streets were crowded and noisy, and there was a lot of hugging and kissing going on, which was okay by me. The four of us ended up in a bar with three girls. Some of the drinks were free to us soldiers, and after a few, we started to feel no pain.

One of the girls fell hard for one from our group named Paul, a big, good-looking guy. She couldn't keep her hands off him. I found a magazine and gave it to the bartender: "Marry these two," I said. I was Paul's best man and had to hold onto him to be able to stand up for him. The couple said their "I do's" and kissed. It was a beautiful wedding, so we all had another drink on the house. Time passed, and we kept saying we should go, but we were having too much fun. Finally, I made a toast to Paul's new wife: "God made you beautiful, God made you sweet, God made you, Gosh I wish I could." And with that, the seven of us headed back to the train station.

When we got to the station and were ready to board, two of the girls kissed us all goodbye and wished us good luck. Paul's girl insisted she was married to him and was going with him. I said to myself, "This is really going to be good."

Sergeant Wicker, our great leader, was very drunk. As we climbed aboard, he managed to count twenty-nine people. It surprised me, because I thought he was too drunk to see. He was having a fit, running up and down the aisles, shouting, "One too many, one too many!" We had told the girl to lie down on one of the bottom bunks to hide.

Suddenly the train began to move. I said to myself, "I think we're in big trouble." Our drunken leader kept insisting there was one too many and kept counting, but he never saw her.

Finally a porter walked by. He didn't say anything, so we figured he hadn't seen her. But he had. He came back with the conductor. The train was moving faster. The conductor told us to move and told the girl, "Get out from the bunk." Then he shouted, "Everyone in this car is under arrest! When we reach Aurora, I'm calling the FBI!"

Sergeant Wicker saw her and yelled, "There's number twenty-nine! Get off the train, Lady!"

"Shut up," the conductor told him. "You're under arrest."

I said to myself, "It may be a few years before I get to see the Seattle Rainiers play baseball again." The other twenty-four guys aboard complained like hell to the conductor. "That's unfair!" they said. "We had nothing to do with it!" They argued and argued.

The girl insisted that she was Paul's wife and had the right to be with him. Paul was so loaded that all he could do was weave back and forth with a stupid grin on his face. Sergeant Wicker kept insisting that she was number twenty-nine and he would personally escort her off the train. The conductor told the sergeant, "You're drunk. Shut up and stay out of it."

Then the conductor, taking complete control of things, said, "I'll give you guys a break. We'll be stopping in Aurora in a few minutes. If you guys will take up a collection and see that this girl has enough for taxi fare back to Chicago, I'll forget the whole thing."

Boy, you have no idea how quickly everyone chipped in. That solution calmed down everyone, except the girl. She hauled off and hit the conductor with her purse, saying, "I'm staying on the train with my husband!" We pulled into Aurora. When we stopped, the porter grabbed one arm and the conductor grabbed the other. She was hollering and screaming, but they managed to get her off the train.

As we pulled away from the station, I could see her crying. Suddenly I felt very sorry for her. It was war time, and she must have been very lonely.

While in Chicago, I had bought a bottle of Southern Comfort for two dollars, to celebrate our great victory. I didn't know what one hundred proof meant, but I found out. When everything got back to normal and we started to sober up, they served dinner. About an hour after dinner, the party started, and I brought out the Southern Comfort....

I remember waking up with a terrible hangover. The click of the wheels on the track actually hurt my head. I heard someone say, "We'll be in Idaho soon."

Back to Civilian Life

Once I returned home from Europe, I had ten days of leave, then reported to Santa Monica, California, for reassignment. I wanted to be assigned to a B-29 bomb group. I just had to fly in one of those super forts. But this was June, 1945. I guess the Air Force figured that with the war almost over, they didn't need any more tail gunners, so they asked me if I wanted to be discharged. My God, civilian life...what would it be like? I couldn't wait to find out.

I was sent back to Fort Lewis to be discharged. I was so excited about becoming a civilian again that, after being interviewed by two newspaper reporters, I couldn't remember a thing about the interviews. I was tired of looking at drab brown uniforms. The next day, I stood on the corner of 45th and University, just watching people walking by, wearing civilian clothes.

I found myself driving around all the old places where I used to hang out with the guys. Green Lake, Wallingford, Lake City, and the Ravenna and Wedgewood areas. And last, the University District, and even though it was June, I remembered it as the most beautifully decorated area of the city at Christmas time. I noticed a gold star hanging in the front window of some of the homes and wondered why. I found out that in that home, a son had been killed in the war. I drove by Jim Casey's house one day. Sure enough, there was a gold star hanging in the window.

I didn't have the guts to go up the steps and visit with his mother, so I waited a few months until Joe Mariani was discharged from the Navy. We went to see her together. When she saw us, she started to cry. It was sad, because without her son she was very much alone. I felt sorry for her, but what could I do? Joe did most of the talking.

When the war was over, I heard that they were going to spare the Japanese emperor. Not only that, but he would be allowed to live in his palace. I was furious. That was the man who had ordered the bombing of Pearl Harbor. What made him better than Hitler or Mussolini? The military brass or the politicians who did not consider the emperor a war criminal probably never lost a son in that war. His people thought he was divine. Then why didn't they ask him to walk on water, or were they afraid to test his spirit?

As far as I was concerned, everyone who fought in the South Pacific, especially those who had lost their lives, were cheated. How about Mrs. Casey? She gave up her only son.

Civilian Work

During the war, when I was stationed in Denver, I had attended a United Airlines school. After finishing the class, they gave me a diploma and told me to show it to the people at UAL in Boeing Field when the war was over, and they would give me a job. They did offer me a job: thirty-five dollars a week, pumping gas into airplanes. Hell, I had just helped win a war! I thought they would offer me at least a junior vice president position. Not to be, so I left. Talk about disappointment!

Leaving Boeing Field, I ended up in the Broadway district. I drove by the Belcourt Studebaker Agency and noticed a one-and-a-half ton Studebaker truck in the showroom. I pulled over, walked into the showroom, and asked the salesman if the truck was for sale. "Ya," he said, "but you have to have a priority." He turned and walked away.

I said, "Well, I'm an honorably discharged veteran."

He turned around quickly and said, "It's all yours! I've been trying to sell this truck for two months. The only ones who qualify are veterans, farmers, or someone else connected with the war effort."

With the help of Sam Picardo, Ernesto's oldest son, and with my three hundred dollars in severance pay, I bought myself a truck for sixteen hundred and forty dollars. Sam and I spent fifty dollars on lumber to build shelves and a flatbed body. We spread linseed oil on the flatbed to preserve the wood. The following Monday, I drove down to Produce Row on Western Avenue.

I backed in front of Rosella Produce Company with six dollars in my pocket. I said to Mike Rosella, "Hey, Mike, I want to start a produce route, but I have to have some credit."

"Take what you want, kid," Mike said. What a guy! I loaded up the truck with fresh produce and, with no customers, headed north. At the end of the week, I added up my sales, subtracted it from my purchases, and I had made one hundred and twenty dollars. I kept checking and double checking. It still came to one hundred and twenty dollars. Unbelievable!

There were about a dozen privately owned produce houses between Madison and Seneca on Western Avenue. I noticed on Produce Row that everyone yelled at one another, everyone swore at one another, everyone lied to one another and finally everyone stole from one another. I said to myself, "This is the life for me."

I did it for fifty years.

Uncle Fred

I have some good memories of family reunions since the war. Some of those memories revolve around Uncle Fred, who moved from Seattle and settled in Orinda, California. He and his family would often visit Seattle. I remember especially the Thanksgiving of 1969. When I knew that Uncle Fred was coming up, I loaded up the freezer with steaks, roasts, chicken and a big ham. Of course, because of my produce business, there were plenty of fresh fruit and vegetables on hand.

Unc would come over to the house around three in the afternoon, clomp downstairs to the freezer and pick out what he wanted to cook for dinner that night. Seattle friends and relatives would call him at our house and say, "Hey Fred, we want you to come over to the house for dinner." His answer was always the same. "Come over to Eddie's house. I'm doing the cooking." Every night we would have a gang. I loved it. He is the only man I know who could eat a dinner while cooking and then eat another one while serving.

We'd have homemade pies, mostly lemon, apple, and Unc's favorite, chocolate. One time I lucked out; the chocolate pie was cooling off, and no one was in the kitchen. I slipped a couple of Ex-Lax in it. I made sure I knew exactly where the Ex-Lax was, so when I cut the pie, my favorite uncle got that piece. The next day he complained, "I spent half the night sitting on the toilet, and boy, am I sore. I guess I ate too much salad."

"I keep telling you to cut down, Unc," I said.

He always called me by my prized nickname, "Asshole." I looked it up in the Webster's Dictionary: *Asshole: a stupid, incompetent, or detestable person.* The Sunday night after Thanksgiving, I drove him to the airport. Just before he boarded the plane with people all around him, he waved at me and yelled, "When you get a chance, come down and visit me, Asshole!" I turned around and pretended he wasn't talking to me. That was the last time I saw him. A few weeks later, he died suddenly of a heart attack. I actually miss being called "Asshole" by Uncle Fred. But I do have good memories of him. Even today, whenever I talk about him, I end up chuckling.

One memory in particular makes me laugh. For Labor Day weekend one year, Uncle Fred and I decided to visit my brother Bob in Las Vegas. After all, Fred and I knew we'd get free room and board at the Golden Gate Casino. I called Bob and told him the good news. But I added, "Bob, please get me a private room. Unc snores so loud, you'd think jets were buzzing the town."

"Okay," Bob said, "but don't you two do anything to embarrass me."

"Fine," I said, "but you tell that to your uncle. I've already been to charm school." I had the feeling our coming down for a visit was not good news to him.

I met Unc in San Francisco, and that night we flew into Vegas. The next morning, I knocked on Unc's hotel room door. He asked, "Who is it?"

In a high pitched voice I replied, "It's the maid!"

He opened the door and shouted, "Oh, it's only you, Asshole!"

We called room service and ordered some hot coffee with butterhorns. We talked about personal things, and about the good old days. Finally I told him I was going to go back to my room to take a shower and would be back in about half an hour. When I left, I secretly changed his door sign that said "Do not Disturb" to "Maid Service." After I showered and dressed, I headed for Unc's room. I walked down the hall.

I saw three Mexican maids. One was red-faced, talking a mile a minute in Spanish, pointing to Uncle Fred's room. I wondered if something was wrong. I rushed to his door and knocked, asking, "Unc, are you all right?"

He opened the door and growled at me, "You turned the sign on the door around, you asshole!"

What had happened, as I found out, was that the maid had knocked on the door, and Unc asked, "Who is it?"

The maid had answered, "It's the maid."

Unc had just gotten out of the shower and had only his bathrobe on. Thinking it was me again, he unlocked the door and said, "Come in." When the maid opened the door, he yelled, "Surprise!" And in a single gesture he flung open his robe; there he stood naked. He said the maid damn near fainted. Unc and Bob never forgave me for that one.

Today

It's been over fifty years since I came back from England. After the war I married and had two beautiful daughters, Tammy and Donna. Tammy is married, has two children, and lives in Las Vegas with her husband, Chuck. Donna graduated from the University of Washington with a 3.47 average. I'm proud of her for that. She is a chip off the old block, a hard worker. She owns and runs a very busy espresso coffee bar at the University Book Store.

My mother is ninety-two years old now. She lives with my sister Norma. Every Tuesday Ma's only living brother, Al, and I go to visit them. We always seem to end up talking about the *good old days*. Norma always cooks us our famous family zucchini and onion frittata, except that she serves it with hash browns. Ma, who always complains, says, "The frittatas that my mother used to cook tasted better!" She plans to be with us for a long time, insisting "If I can't take it with me, I'm not going!"

I still visit Joe Mariani in the same house where I met him sixty-three years ago. Joe was always a very generous man...today he lets me cut his grass! But I don't mind, because his wife, Alice, makes good biscotti.

I used to drive right by Joe's house on NE 80th very early in the morning, on my way to pick up produce. I'd tack a "FOR SALE" sign to his house. When I was finished with my route, I'd double back, invite myself in for coffee, and listen to Joe and his family argue with one another about who put the sign on the house. Naturally, I would put in my two cents, telling them, "It had to be a real estate company that could profit from the sale!" I'd do this about every six months.

Bob moved to Las Vegas in the 1950s. Soon he became general manager and part owner of the Golden Gate Casino at #1 Fremont Street in downtown Las Vegas. He spent a lot of his precious vacation time in Seattle visiting the family. He loved coming on my produce route with me. Once we were on the route, he would say to me, "Now Eddie, let me get this straight again. You bought a truck for sixteen hundred and forty dollars, built a body on it for fifty bucks, and you were in business."

I'd say, "That's right."

"You know," he'd say, "with the exception of the truck, the only overhead you have is the order book in your back pocket. Do you have any idea what it cost us to start The Golden Gate?" They had three hundred employees at the time.

I would say, "Bob, what I make in a year, you make in a week, possibly a lot more."

But Bob liked the hard physical work associated with delivering produce. He would answer, "Yeah, but you're lucky; you get for free what I've got to go to a gym and pay for."

When he and Joe would come on the route, they'd spend so much time talking to the customers that when we got toward the end of the route, I'd tell the last customers, "I could have been here two hours earlier, but—" pointing to Joe and Bob—"my help showed up."

Even though he loved the idea of the produce route, Bob tried for years to get me to quit the route and move down to Vegas. "You can make a lot more money," he said.

I told him, "I love this route, and I'm having fun. Besides, there's no way I would ever leave beautiful Seattle."

Bob was always offering me money. But I'd say, "No, you're my ace in the hole. If I ever need anything, I've got you to come to." That was a good feeling.

I'd tell people the reason Bob had so much money was every time he'd visit Seattle, he'd take over the route and just before he left, I'd have to buy it back.

Birthdays in July

My fondest memory of Bob was back in July of 1972, the year I turned fifty. There were about twelve of us who had birthdays in July, some relatives and some close friends. That July we planned to have the big communal birthday party at the home of our friends, Dick and Louise. They had a beautiful home north of Seattle. Dick's birthday was also in July.

A few days before the party, Bob and I dropped off a box of fruit and vegetables for Louise, who was cooking the birthday dinner. We visited for a while, and as we left, I managed to walk out with a beautiful icon from their fireplace mantel. When Bob found out, he had a fit.

"Why did you do that!" he shouted. "They'll notice it's missing and call the police."

"Don't worry," I said calmly. "We'll give it to Dick for his birthday. They'll never miss it before then. They've got too much stuff on their fireplace, anyway."

So we had the icon beautifully wrapped. That Saturday evening, we slipped it in with the rest of the gifts. There were about sixty of us at the party. The home had a large deck with a beautiful backyard. Most of the people were in the backyard, and a few were on the deck. This gave us a chance to cause some trouble inside.

Dick and Louise had their own private bedrooms, so Bob and I decided that we could switch their clothes from one bedroom to the other without being caught. We had to keep our eyes open down the hallway, with the kitchen on one side and the living room on the other. We didn't want anyone around when we crossed the hallway with their clothes in our arms. In the meantime, we would occasionally stroll out to the backyard to socialize, so we wouldn't be missed. Well, it took us over two hours, and it was hard work, but we managed. I thought we did a good job.

After dinner, they finally started opening up the gifts. Bob and I handed Dick our gift. We told him we thought he was a very special guy, and he deserved to have it. He said, "Thanks guys. It sure is beautifully wrapped." When he opened it, he pulled the icon out of the box and said, "Oh, we have something exactly like this on our fireplace."

When Louise looked at the mantel, she started to scream. It wasn't until that moment that she noticed the icon was missing. Then she saw that it was a practical joke, and she started yelling at Bob and me.

"Louise," I said calmly, "you should be glad we didn't break it."

Dick laughed, "Even though you're a couple of crooks, I still like having you around."

Later that evening, I realized that Bob and I were the only two in the house. We were sitting in the living room, but everyone else was in the front yard. Then I heard people yelling, "Hey Eddie, come out here!"

I told Bob, "I'm not going out there! They must have found out that we switched their clothes, and they're going to turn the sprinkler system on me!" Bob just sat there and said nothing.

Finally they came in and dragged me out. There in the driveway was the most beautiful blue and silver two-and-a-half-ton Chevrolet truck with a sixteen-foot, custom-made body on it, with sliding doors on both sides of the body. It was Bob's gift to me for my fiftieth birthday. I was stunned. I went back in the house. Bob was still sitting in the living room. I tried to ask, "Why?" but no words came out. I tried to say, "Thank you," but still no words.

I drove the truck home that night, parked it in front of the house, and just stared at it. Then the phone rang, and it was Louise. She made it clear that I would never be invited to her house again. I didn't mind. It was about the tenth time she had told me that, and I knew she was teasing. I told her I'd go down to Skid Row in the morning and pay a couple of guys to switch her clothes back. She said, "Don't you dare!" I'm still invited over to her house. She is a beautiful woman and boy, can she cook.

I loved my truck. The only guys I would allow to drive it were Bob and a close friend, Frank Falsini, who would take the route for me so I could take off for a few days. Now I understand why Edgar Spencer would not give up his shot-up bomber. Something like that becomes a part of you. I drove it for fourteen years, had a new engine put in it, and never once put so much as a dent in it.

My Best Friend

In 1981 we were very concerned about Bob; he was losing weight and had been seeing a doctor. On April 6 of that year, at 6:30 in the evening, I got a call from Bob. He said all his tests were in, and he had cancer of the esophagus and liver (even though he never drank). "I'm terminal," he said. "They give me six months."

"Oh no!" I remember saying in a low voice, too shocked to say anything more. I started to cry, so I told Bob I would call him back. I locked myself in the bath-room. I didn't want anyone to see how I felt and just cried and cried. I realized I had to compose myself, but it took a good half hour.

I managed to call Bob back, asking what I could do. He said, "Nothing. I've got enough money to travel anywhere in the world for a cure, but there is no cure." I felt so sorry for Bob, but worse, there was nothing I could do for him. For the next few weeks, I ran my produce business in a daze, but I managed. Saying a complete rosary for Bob every day, I felt sure of a miracle. I have always persevered in prayer, learning that God can be silent for years and can say, "No." Then again, maybe I don't recognize that He has given me my answers.

But on December 30, 1981, my niece Linda called me from Las Vegas and told me that Bob had died peacefully, just as my Grandma had. Saints always die peacefully. He was only fifty-eight years old. Again, I locked myself in the bathroom and cried. Nothing is more expensive then losing the ones you love.

The Dream

About a month after the bombing of Pearl Harbor I had a dream. I dreamt that I was sitting on the back porch of my Great Uncle Sabino's house. All of a sudden, I saw coming from the east a cloud. As it got closer I noticed a beautiful woman in the cloud. I said to myself, "Oh my God, it's the Blessed Virgin Mary. I'm in for it. What did I do wrong?"

As it got closer, though, I saw it was my grandmother. She came close to me and said, "If you will pray, everything will be all right."

Then I saw a man in a trench or a ditch, holding a sledge hammer. Above were three Japanese soldiers with rifles in their hands, with their fingers on the trigger. The rifles had bayonets, and the three lunged forward to kill the man.

The man swung the sledge hammer and killed all three soldiers. I figured it signified the power of prayer. I jumped up in bed wide awake and shouted, "How is this possible?" I started to cry, thinking that my grandmother had been in the room. If only I had awakened earlier, I thought, I could have kept her here with me. Then I realized it was a dream. It took a while to fall back to sleep.

I thought about it again the next morning, but then I forgot all about it, until I started flying as a tail gunner. When I flew my second bombing mission and wanted to double my insurance, it was because I had no intention of quitting. The way my dad had called me names when I was young made me feel dirty; I had low self-esteem. But this time, I wanted to do something to make myself proud, even if it cost me my life. There is not one of us who does not seek approval. It was then that I remembered the dream and started saying the rosary.

In all the years since I had the dream, I never told anyone about it. I honestly thought no one would believe me.

When Bob died, I took it very hard. He had been my very best friend, and I missed him. A couple of weeks after he died, I was driving down the freeway to load up my produce for the day. It was early morning. I said to myself, "Death is so permanent. It would be nice if we got one postcard from the dead, with two words on it, like, 'With God,' 'In Heaven,' 'I'm happy.' " Suddenly, I felt as though someone hit me hard on the chest to get my attention. I didn't hear or see anything, but I *felt* two words: "Keep praying." And I knew it was from my brother Bob.

All of a sudden, a great joy came over me, because I knew that he was with Grandmother. How else could he have said, "Keep praying"? I had never told anyone about the dream.

I think of Grandma and Bob often. Sometimes tears fill my eyes. Sometimes I smile and laugh. I'm *sure* I will be with them someday. I've been told more than once that I'll never get to heaven, because there is too much hell in me. That's okay; I'm going to make it. I'll bet Grandma has got a tunnel already built for her favorite grandson, just in case. I may have to crawl on my hands and knees to get in, but I'll make it.

I am a survivor.

ORDER FORM

Qty.	Title	Price	Can. Price	Total
	TALES OF A TAIL GUNNER	**$14.95**	**$17.95**	
	Shipping and handling (add $3.00 for first book, $2.00 for each additonal book)			
	Sales tax (WA residents only, add 8.2%)			
	Total enclosed			

Telephone Orders:
Call (800) 461-1931
Have your VISA or
MasterCard ready.

Fax Orders:
(206) 672-8597
Fill out order
blank and fax.

Postal Orders:
Hara Publishing
P.O. Box 19732
Seattle, WA 98109

Payment:Please Check One

☐ Check

☐ VISA

☐ MasterCard

Expiration Date:_____/_____

Card #:_____

Name on Card:_____

Name_____

Address_____

City_____ **State**_____ **Zip**_____

Daytime Phone(_____**)**_____

Quantity discounts are available.
For more information, call (206) 776-3390.

Thank you for your order!

I understand that I may return any books for a full refund
if not satisfied